99 2019 Fantasy Baseball Player Debates

Written by Chris Welsh and Scott Bogman

Special thanks to ITL Army Members JAG and Jesse Severe for their help!

Thank you for buying our Book! We have been known for our 'Player Debates' on the ITL Fantasy Baseball Podcast for awhile, and feel like this is a reflection of our inner monologue when deciding between players. We don't expect agreement on the arguments of course, as everyone will have their own opinions, but it is always interesting to hear the side of the player you don't want in the debate. We hope this will help you with the players involved in the debates, overall draft strategy and add to your fantasy baseball knowledge!

Things you need to know for the book We are basing this on standard 5x5, 12 man, H2H leagues. These debates sometimes are straight up, positional or who you should take according to their draft positions. We don't necessarily agree with the players that we were assigned on every debate but we argue them anyway!

Our guest judges are using a boxing scoring scale to cast their vote. A "Draw" by a judge or a "Draw" decision represents a split. A "10-7" means the debate is heavily in favor of that side. "A 10-8" is a debate that has some back and forth, but still clearly in favor of that side of the debate. A "10-9" represents a very close match, but in the end just falls on the side of that debate. A "KO or knockout" represents a no brainer win for that side of the debate.

We would love to hear what you guys like about this book, what we should add for next year or what interesting player debates you have. We have an insider program called the ITL Army. It's at Patreon.com/ITLArmy. We will be doing a special book related podcast for Army members only. The episode will cover your questions, debates you wanted to see and more.

Contact Us
Scott Bogman - @BogmanSports, Bogman@InThisLeague.com
Chris Welsh - @IsitTheWelsh, TheWelsh@InThisLeague.com

Be sure to check out the In This League Fantasy Baseball Podcast at www.InThisLeague.com

Special Guest Judges

Alex Chamberlain
RotoGraphs, @DolphHauldhagen

Chris Blessing
Baseball HQ, @C_Blessing

Chris Meaney
The Athletic, @chrismeaney

Clay Link
Rotowire / Sirius XM, @ClayWLink

Derek Van Riper
Rotowire, @DerekVanRiper

Eddy Almaguer
Prospects Live, @EddyAlmaguer

Eno Sarris
The Athletic, @EnoSarris

Jake Ciely
The Athletic, @allinkid

James Anderson
Rotowire, @RealJRAnderson

Jason Collette
Rotowire / ESPN / Fangraphs / UCF, @JasonCollette

Joe Pisapia
Author of The Fantasy Black Book, @JoePisapia17

KC Bubba
FantasySportsDegens.com / Benched With Bubba, @bdentrek

Matt Modica
CTM Baseball, @CTMbaseball

Nathan Grimm
Rotoworld, @Nate_Grimm

Nick Pollack
Pitcher List, @PitcherList

Paul Sporer
Fangraphs, @Sporer

Rob Silver
Baseball Prospectus / Launch Angle Podcast, @RobSilver

Ryan Bloomfield
BaseballHQ, @RyanBHQ

Sammy Reid
Rotogrinders, @SammyReidFI

Steve Gardner
USA Today, @SteveAGardner

Tim Heaney
Rotowire / ESPN, @Tim_Heaney

Stats Abbreviations

Hitters

AB - At Bats
AVG - Batting Average
BB - Walks
BABIP - Batting Average on Balls In Play
Contact% - Contact Percentage
H- Hits
Hard% - Hard Contact Percentage
HR - Home Run
HR/FB - Home Run to Fly Ball Percentage
ISO - Isolated Power
Med% - Medium Contact Percentage
OBP - On Base Percentage
OPS - On Base plus Slugging Percentage
PA - Plate Appearances
R - Runs Scored
RBI - Runs Batted In
SB - Stolen Base
Soft% - Soft Contact Percentage
SwStr - Swinging Strike Rate
XBH - Extra Base Hits

Pitchers

BB - Walks
BB/9 - Walks per 9 innings
CG - Complete Game
ER - Earned Runs
ERA - Earn Runs Average
FB% - Fly Ball Percentage
GB% - Ground Ball percentage
GS - Games Started
IP - Innings Pitched
K - Strikeouts
K% - Strikeout Percentage
K/9 - Strikeouts per 9 innings
LD - Line Drive Percentage
LOB% - Left on Base Percentage
QS - Quality Start
SO - Shutout
SV - Saves
W - Win
WHIP - Walks and Hits Per Inning Pitched
FIP - Fielding Independent Pitching
xFIP - Expected Fielding Independent Pitching

Fight Card

MIKE **TROUT** VS THE **FIELD**

	MIKE TROUT			THE FIELD	
AVG.	.312	★	AVG.	.310	
HR	39	★	HR	38	
RBI	79		★ RBI	103	
RUNS	101		★ RUNS	119	
SB	24	★	SB	23	

ROUND 1

MIKE TROUT

BOGMAN

Last year, I made the argument that the field beats Trout, and to be honest, that's usually true. But it's really hard to find a more consistent performer than Trout on a year-to-year basis. Over the last three seasons, his lows are a .306 average, 92 runs, 29 home runs, 72 driven in, and 22 swipes, and most of those stats were from his 2017 season during which he missed 48 games. There are certainly some strong pitching options, but no one is going to take a pitcher over a hitter unless you are in a points league. The only real argument is for Mookie Betts. He has had a similar three-year stretch to Trout, but Trout has been at the top of the class for seven straight seasons. Lindor is great but has hit in the .270-.280 range the past two seasons. José Ramírez has only two years of consistency under his belt and also hit in the .270 range. Altuve has been banged up and the stolen base totals have gone down. Arenado has the consistency but doesn't steal bases. Yelich has only one year of greatness. Manny Machado and Bryce Harper do everything but are wildly inconsistent in average and steals. Year in and year out, Trout provides us consistent first round value, this year will be no different. Trout goes the distance with The Field and emerges victorious.

THE FIELD

THE WELSH

Ah, yes! The old "insert player over Mike Trout" debate. It makes sense since Trout hasn't finished as the #1 overall fantasy player in three years. In standard 5x5, he's finished inside the top ten twice while the other was a top thirty finish. The field certainly is fun and all, but the real question is, "Who warrants being taken a head of Trout?" Only two players come to mind: Mookie Betts and José Ramírez. Starting with J.R., he's the only one of these three who has finished inside the top twenty each of the past two years while amassing the largest home run growth from one season to the next (29 in 2017 to 39 in 2018). Mookie on the other hand has finished as the #1 overall fantasy player two of the last three seasons. He is the only one of these three with three straight 100+ run seasons. Additionally, Betts has accumulated the most combined stolen bases over the last three years (82), six more than Trout during the same timeframe. These three provide consistent production in all categories. J.R. trended up over the last two years with a position advantage. Mookie rank-wise has finished as the best over the last three years. Factoring in the crop of upcoming talent to rival these spots which may be better than any previous year, it might be ok to take Mookie or José. Don't get crazy though...

WINNER - DRAW ★ ★ ★

20 19

IN THIS LEAGUE — FANTASY SPORTS PODCAST NETWORK

Judges Scorecard

STEVE GARDNER	JAKE CIELY	JASON COLLETTE
FIELD 10-9	**DRAW**	**TROUT 10-9**

Round 1: Mike Trout vs The Field

MOOKIE BETTS $\overline{\text{VS}}$ JOSÉ RAMÍREZ

	MOOKIE BETTS				JOSÉ RAMÍREZ	
AVG.	.346	★		AVG.		.270
HR	32			★ HR		39
RBI	80			★ RBI		105
RUNS	129	★		RUNS		110
SB	30			★ SB		34

ROUND 2

MOOKIE BETTS

THE WELSH

Well hello, Mr. Betts! I just made the case for these two over Trout. Now, let me go further into making the case for Betts over J.R. aside from two #1 overall fantasy finishes during the last three seasons and not including the higher number of runs and stolen bases over that same timeframe. I also don't need to mention Betts won a 2018 batting title and was the first to ever do it while also posting a 30/30 season. I could mention only two players in 2018 hit .300 and stole 30 bases (Betts and Cain), but would that be fair? If I wanted to, I can throw out the four players that hit .300 and had 30 or more home runs, but it wouldn't be fair since Jose Ramirez isn't on that list with Betts (FYI, J.D. Martinez, Trout and Christian Yelich are the others). The truth is: we're trying to pick our favorite child. Both are great. Ramírez's 2018 100-100-30-30 season was remarkable, but it was at the cost of his batting average dipping forty points from the previous two seasons to .270. In 5x5, Betts won the battle and keeps the title of MVP! I guess I did mention that.

JOSÉ RAMÍREZ

BOGMAN

There were three major differences from last year's production between these two. Mookie had the advantage in batting average (.346 to .270). Ramírez had 25 more runs batted in than Mookie (105-80). Betts had 19 more runs scored than Ramírez (129-110). Mookie was the league leader in batting average among qualified hitters and also was tied for the league lead in runs scored. I'm just not that convinced that these numbers are repeatable. Mookie improved his average 82 points from 17' to 18'. This was partially credited to his improved hard-hit ball percentage, which was raised from 35.8% in 2017 to 44.5% in 2018. José Ramírez, on the other hand, raised his hard-hit percentage to 36.1% which was a career high. Ramírez has raised his hard-hit percentage for all five seasons he has been in "The Bigs." BABIP is also a big factor in the difference in batting average for these two. Mookie had a 100-point increase from 2017 to 2018, which made sense as a result of the increased hard-hit percentage, but I think it's reasonable to expect some regression. José lost 67 points in BABIP even with the increased hard-hit percentage. So, we can expect an increase in batting average for him. With the batting averages evening out I'll lean towards Ramírez with the 3B eligibility. In a hard-fought bout, José Ramírez wins in a majority decision.

★ ★ ★ WINNER - MOOKIE BETTS 10-9 ★ ★ ★

20 19

Judges Scorecard

JOE PISAPIA	DEREK VAN RIPER	RYAN BLOOMFIELD
BETTS 10-9	BETTS 10-9	BETTS 10-8

Round 2: Mookie Betts vs José Ramírez

RONALD ACUNA VS BRYCE HARPER

RONALD ACUNA				BRYCE HARPER	
AVG.	.293 ★		AVG.		.249
HR	26		★ HR		34
RBI	64	**ROUND 3**	★ RBI		100
RUNS	78		★ RUNS		103
SB	16 ★		SB		13

RONALD ACUÑA

THE WELSH

Ronald Acuña! Wow! We're already squaring him up against Bryce Harper?!?! New home in 2019 or not, Harper has always produced. His main problem: inconsistent performance. His average has swung sixty to ninety points between seasons. The only consistent thing about his average is it's inconsistent. Some years, he gets the green light on the base paths and some he doesn't run at all. Home runs, runs batted in and runs are a lock for Bryce, but what about the other two? Harper has averaged 26 home runs and 10.7 stolen bases per season during his career and has seen an increase to almost 13 swipes per season during last three years. In Acuña's first major league season, he tied Harper's career home run average and surpassed his stolen base average. Steamer projects Acuña to accumulate 29 home runs and 26 stolen bases. In 2019, only four players hit those marks: Betts, Ramírez, Trevor Story and Francisco Lindor. Acuña hit .293 last year and is projected to hit .279 in 2019, which is still thirteen points higher than Harper's 2019 projected batting average. You may sacrifice a few of the elite big three categories Harper consistently gives you, but Acuña's bump in stolen bases pushes him into one of the handful of true 5-tool players in the game right now. Acuña shocks the world!

BRYCE HARPER

BOGMAN

I can't believe it's difficult to defend Bryce Harper against a 2nd year player but Ronald Acuña Jr is that good. Acuña was really incredible in his rookie debut and he got better as the season went on hitting .322 in the second half versus .249 in the first half. Acuña's first year actually looked a lot like Harper's rookie season, both won rookie of the year and showed an impeccable power/speed combo that everyone was drooling over. Now it's true that Bryce Harper never stole 40+ bases in the minors, but to be fair he didn't have to spend more than one season in the minors. We have seen plenty of ups and downs in Harper's career but the floor is so much higher than almost everyone else he's an easy 1st round pick in almost every draft. Harper has runs, HRs, RBI on lock over the last 4 years his lows are 84, 24 and 86. Harper's SBs are probably not going to match Acuña's. The batting average for Harper has taken wild swings from as high as .330 to as low as .243 and those were in back to back seasons. I won't preach sophomore slump for Acuña or anything but I will say that I don't think Harper has reached his potential and he already has an MVP and 6 all star appearances.

★ ★ ★ **WINNER - BRYCE HARPER 10-9** ★ ★ ★

2019

Judges Scorecard

NICK POLLACK	PAUL SPORER	ROB SILVER
HARPER 10-9	HARPER 10-9	ACUÑA 10-8

Round 3: Ronald Acuña vs Bryce Harper

MAX SCHERZER VS CHRIS SALE

	MAX SCHERZER			ROUND 4		CHRIS SALE	
WINS	18 ★				WINS	12	
ERA	2.53			★	ERA	2.11	
WHIP	0.911			★	WHIP	0.861	
K	300 ★				K	237	
IP	220.2 ★				IP	158.0	

MAX SCHERZER

THE WELSH

Max is everything that is great about baseball. He hasn't pitched fewer than 200 innings in a season since 2012. He's struck out more than 200 batters in every season since 2012. Did I mention 2018 was his career high in strikeouts at 300 at the age of 34? Ultimately, these guys are very similar: super human aces at the top of their game and most likely two of the top three pitchers taken this upcoming season. Sale's pure stuff always seems to be the best of the best. Take last season during which he led all pitchers with 150 innings or more pitched in K%, K/9 and BB/K%. He strikes fools out, and that's just what we want in fantasy. He's even had a had a better K/9 than Scherzer in four of the last five years. Did you know though Scherzer has more actual strikeouts than Sale in every single season but one since 2012? It comes down to staying on the field. Remember the 200-innings statistic for Max? Sale has 200+ innings in only three of his last five seasons. 2018 was his lowest since 2011. Let me throw in the ol' AL versus NL argument and factor in the difficulty of the divisions in which they pitch. It's fun to dream with Sale, but when making that big of a commitment to draft pitching early, Max is the clear cut consistent option for five years running. Scherzer with a 7th round knockout which turns one of Sale's eye a different color.

CHRIS SALE

BOGMAN

The first thing that jumps out in this debate is that Chris Sale only threw 158 innings to Scherzer's 220. Sale sustained a shoulder injury in 2018, and upon his return, he was overthrowing a little bit. In doing so, he didn't do any permanent or "real" damage but did experience lingering shoulder soreness. The soreness scared the Red Sox into implementing the Rays "Opener" on occasion with him, and they simply would not allow him to pitch deep into games towards the end of the season. My guess would be that Sale didn't really know how to deal with an injury to his shoulder because this was his first actual injury as he hadn't missed a start since 2015...2015! In any case, it was a Grade I (mild) strain resulting in no surgery and requiring Sale to rest during the offseason to heal the inflammation. While Sale's totals didn't match up to Scherzer's, the underlying numbers were better in K/9 (13.50 for Sale; 12.24 for Scherzer) BB/9 (1.94 for Sale; 2.08 for Scherzer), and xFIP (2.31 for Sale; 3.08 for Scherzer). Despite the setbacks, Sale still bested Scherzer in ERA and WHIP. These guys have been at the top of the draft list for pitchers for a very long time, and this season is no different. If your draft is before spring training and you don't want the injury risk in Sale, it is understandable. If Sale is participating and looks healthy at the time of your draft, then the underlying numbers have him by a slight edge. In another split decision, the southpaw defeats Scherzer in a battle of two of the best.

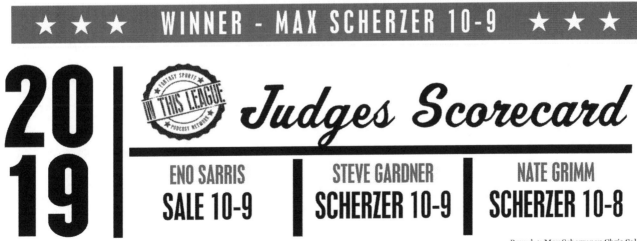

★ ★ ★ WINNER - MAX SCHERZER 10-9 ★ ★ ★

2019 IN THIS LEAGUE Judges Scorecard

ENO SARRIS	STEVE GARDNER	NATE GRIMM
SALE 10-9	SCHERZER 10-9	SCHERZER 10-8

Round 4: Max Scherzer vs Chris Sale

FRANSICO LINDOR VS JOSÉ ALTUVE

	LINDOR		ROUND 5		ALTUVE
AVG.	.277			★ AVG.	.316
HR	38 ★			HR	13
RBI	92 ★			RBI	61
RUNS	129 ★			RUNS	84
SB	35 ★			SB	17

FRANCISCO LINDOR

THE WELSH

329 Runs, 86 HR, 259 RBI, 59 SB

304 Runs, 61 HR, 239 RBI, 79 SB

The top stat line is Lindor's three-year totals, and the bottom three-year totals belong to Altuve. The point of looking comparing this numbers will add to the argument in favor of Altuve that 2018 was an off year. While I don't fully disagree, one would have to factor in an arbitrary production percentage (let's say 10%) for Altuve to rebound and once again separate from the pack. One key is the trajectory these two players have been moving over these last three years. Lindor has improved each year over the last three years in home runs, runs, and runs batted in. From 2017 to 2018, Lindor saw improvements in both stolen bases and batting average. On the other hand, Altuve has seen declines during the last three seasons in runs batted in as well as a dip in stolen bases, runs and home runs during the past season. While this isn't all about devolving and evolving players, Altuve isn't coming at enough of a discount anymore to warrant drafting him above Lindor. The first five rounds are hard fought, but the youth takes over with a power right from Lindor for a 6th round KO.

JOSÉ ALTUVE

BOGMAN

Altuve will be a tough sell here because Lindor had an incredible 2018 season, while Altuve was banged up at the end of the season and playing through it. The big question is, "What is actually repeatable for Lindor?" He had career highs in four of five categories, and his HR/FB rate was much higher than it has ever been. I may have to concede the fact he might just be rounding into his potential because he is still only 25 years old. Do keep in mind 25 of his bombs came in the first half, AND he hit 35 points lower in the second half of the season. The dip in average is most likely because he hit only .251 against the shift, which increased in frequency during the second half. Altuve had some weird splits as well and played much better in the first half, but his second half struggles can be tied to his late July knee injury, which kept him on the DL until August 21st. While Altuve gutted it out in the second half of the season, he was definitely not 100% as he only hit .276 down the stretch (50 points below his career average). Altuve had surgery, will be 100% for spring training, and back to hitting third for one of the best lineups with Springer and Bregman ahead of him and Correa and Brantley behind him. A healthy Altuve versus Lindor coming off a career year is tough, but I'll take Altuve in a split decision.

★ ★ ★ WINNER - FRANCISCO LINDOR 10-8 ★ ★ ★

2019

Judges Scorecard

PAUL SPORER	ALEX CHAMBERLAIN	JASON COLLETTE
LINDOR 10-8	LINDOR 10-8	LINDOR 10-8

Round 5: Francisco Lindor vs José Altuve

NOLAN ARENADO — VS — KRIS BRYANT

	NOLAN ARENADO			KRIS BRYANT
AVG.	.297 ★	ROUND 6	AVG.	.272
HR	38 ★		HR	13
RBI	110 ★		RBI	52
RUNS	104 ★		RUNS	59
SB	2		SB	2

NOLAN ARENADO

BOGMAN

Kris Bryant is going to be a hell of a deal this season. There's no doubting that. We need to remember why he is coming at a two-round discount from where Nolan Arenado is being drafted. He had an awful year based where he was being drafted. Yes, we can blame the awful year on the problematic shoulder because it was almost definitely the culprit. My issue with drafting Bryant is he didn't have the shoulder repaired but rather just rested it during the off-season. Then, he started hitting again in January. Surgery might have eaten into his 2019 campaign, but it would have almost certainly taken care of the injury. Rest can absolutely work for the injury, but this is what we also thought for Josh Donaldson going into last season and all know how that worked out. Arenado is expensive. He will go in the first half of the first round in almost every single draft, but Arenado might be the surest bet of anyone. During his four seasons, his lows in runs, homers, runs driven in and batting average are 97, 37, 110 and .287 respectively. On top of those astounding numbers, he also plays in the best home ballpark for hitters and shows no signs of slowing down at all. Simply said, Kris Bryant is still a costly roll of the dice while Arenado is anything but that. Arenado wins in a TKO in his fourth straight season finishing in the top five of the MVP voting.

KRIS BRYANT

THE WELSH

It's no secret 'round these parts I'm what you might call a "fan" of Kris Bryant. There might be some "legal terms" some jurisdictions choose to use, but that's beside the point. 2018 Bryant vs 2018 Arenado is laughable! They don't live in the same dimension. The question becomes based on the price tag, "Can Bryant win this?" Let's start with the injuries. Bryant was hit in the head, shoulder, and hand resulting in 102 games played. Every tangible fantasy stat line was a career low. Taking a deeper look, Bryant had his second worst strikeout percentage since his rookie season (23.4%) and had a career high in soft contact percentage (18.9%), 4% higher than 2017. His HR/FB rate was 7.5% lower than his career 2016 year. He stunk, right? It's hard overlook that injuries didn't play a huge role. Higher strikeouts, softer contact, and muted power... a rebound is coming. I guarantee it! Steamer projects Bryant with more runs than Arenado in 2019 and within striking distance in both home runs and batting average. I won't say draft Bryant over Arenado, but when factoring in the late second round/early third round value for Bryant versus a top 6 overall pick for Arenado, it would allow you to focus on steals early on while grabbing Arenado-like numbers a few rounds later. Bryant with a 12 round 10-9 win.

★ ★ ★ WINNER - NOLAN ARENADO 10-9 ★ ★ ★

20 19

Judges Scorecard

ROB SILVER	JOE PISAPIA	SAMMY REID
ARENADO 10-7	ARENADO 10-8	BRYANT KO

Round 6: Nolan Arenado vs Kris Bryant

ALEX BREGMAN VS ANDREW BENINTENDI

	ALEX BREGMAN				ANDREW BENINTENDI
AVG.	.286			AVG.	.290
HR	31 ★			HR	16
RBI	103 ★	ROUND 7		RBI	87
RUNS	105 ★			RUNS	103
SB	10		★	SB	21

ALEX BREGMAN

THE WELSH

Pop quiz: How many guys had a HR/SB season of 15+/20+ in 2018? 11. How many had a HR/SB season of 30+/10+ in 2018? 9. I don't know about you, but I'd have said for sure the 30/10 season was much more common than the type of power coming from someone swiping 20+ bases. We're always chasing stolen bases, but the numbers are rising. In fact, 30+ home runs is the new 20+ stolen bases. 28 players stole 20 or more bases in 2018, while only 27 hit 30 or more home runs. Now let's talk about what really makes Alex Bregman so special. Contact? I know you're asking, "But Welsh! Benintendi had a higher average!" Correct sir, but the stuff under the hood for Bregman have me leaning towards the idea the best is still yet to come. Bregman was fourth in baseball in contact on balls outside the zone (O-Contact%) and thirteenth in baseball on contact on balls inside the zone (Z-Contact%). Bregman's 2018 season was a true 5-tool fantasy season. 20+-100+-100+-10+ and a .280 or higher average is a baseline for a five-star fantasy player. Steamer projections temper some of Bregman's 2018, but I think last year's numbers are very repeatable. Plus, add on the extra year of shortstop eligibility. Bregman and Benintendi look like equal foes, but Bregman wins in an early round KO.

ANDREW BENINTENDI

BOGMAN

The 2015 draft and then the 2016 call to the majors have kept these two linked together and probably will for the rest of their careers. This season though the value is about at the very least a round different in most situations so this is more about where we are drafting these guys than it has been the past two seasons. As I am typing this, these guys are separated by 18 spots in NFBC drafting: Bregman is going at 11 and Benintendi is at 29. Bregman definitely had the better 2018 season but still only edged out Beni by one category in a traditional 5x5 league. 15 homers and 16 driven in versus 11 swipes is the big difference between these guys with the Benintendi getting the edge in runs by two and batting average by .004. If we're looking at scarcity of these stats, the simple answer is the stolen bases are worth more as there's one stolen base for every 2.25 bombs hit and one steal to every 8.3 run batted in. Now of course, it's not that simple. We have seen Bregman display the ability to steal bases, and it's hard to ignore his power surge from last season. On the other side of the coin, Benintendi will be hitting leadoff and get plenty of stolen base opportunities AND he is a round cheaper. If I can select someone more established where Bregman is being drafted and get Benintendi later, that's how I would approach this one. This bout goes to the scorecards with Beni Biceps edging out Bregman.

★ ★ ★ WINNER - ALEX BREGMAN 10-9 ★ ★ ★

2019 | IN THIS LEAGUE | *Judges Scorecard*

STEVE GARDNER	DEREK VAN RIPER	CHRIS MEANEY
10-9 BREGMAN	10-9 BREGMAN	10-8 BREGMAN

Round 7: Alex Bregman vs Andrew Benintendi

BLAKE SNELL VS CLAYTON KERSHAW

	BLAKE SNELL				CLAYTON KERSHAW
WINS	21 ★			WINS	9
ERA	1.89 ★	ROUND		ERA	2.73
WHIP	0.974 ★	8		WHIP	1.041
K	221 ★			K	155
IP	180.2 ★			IP	161.1

BLAKE SNELL
BOGMAN

I couldn't believe it when I saw that Snell is going ahead of Kershaw in early NFBC drafts. The fact is people are more willing to take a risk on a one year wonder in Snell, than an injury prone great in Kershaw. I can say without hesitation that if we were guaranteed to get a full season out of Kershaw he would be the pick, he's one of the best lefties ever, his ERA hasn't been over 3 since his rookie season, his WHIP has been over one twice in the past 8 seasons and he is unbelievably dominant when he's out there. Kershaw just isn't dependable anymore and last season it started to affect his strikeout numbers as his K/9 dipped to 8.65 which was the lowest he's had since his rookie season and the first time it dipped below 10 since 2013. Blake Snell is in line for some regression for sure but the first season he gets a full run at it he wins the AL Cy Young Award, led the league in wins, was 2nd in ERA, gave up the fewest runs among qualified starters, 4th in WHIP, and 10th in strikeouts. Even with some regression it looks like Snell is heading into a long successful career and Kershaw is going to continue to miss games with chronic back issues. If I'm betting on one of these guys it's definitely going to be Snell.

CLAYTON KERSHAW
THE WELSH

I think we have seen some key indicators that Snell is going to regress, but with respect to last season, he's far from falling off the cliff. Snell had the highest LOB% in the last five years (career average is 77%) and a difference of about 1.5 runs from his ERA to xFIP. He also produced lowest BABIP of the top thirty qualified pitchers in ERA in 2018. I'm not calling for him to not be worth a top 10 pitcher spot, but he is going to regress. Kershaw already has regressed over the last few years. A positive note is the very public comment regarding Kershaw focusing on getting his back right and regaining velocity during the 2018-19 offseason. My key here is the acceptance of this opportunity and not fighting against it. His fastball velocity dropped to a career low of 90.9. Interestingly enough, Justin Verlander at the age of 30 saw his velocity drop to a career low of 92.3. Verlander began moving his slider to a cutter in 2017, and not only did his strikeouts and effectiveness rise, so did his velocity (now up to 95.1 on average). I'm not saying Kershaw will mirror Verlander, but he is openly talking about working on his health and velocity in the off-season. We have a similar test case in Verlander. He signed an incentive based contract extension in which he is betting on himself. A focus on the fastball and health is something I will bet on over the one-year performance of Snell. They are closer than ever before, but give me the discount on Kershaw. Kershaw in a 10-8 12-round victory.

★ ★ ★ WINNER - BLAKE SNELL 10-8 ★ ★ ★

20 19 | Judges Scorecard

JAMES ANDERSON	ENO SARRIS	JASON COLLETTE
SNELL 10-8	SNELL 10-8	SNELL 10-9

Round 8: Blake Snell vs Clayton Kershaw

CHRISTIAN YELICH VS J.D. MARTINEZ

	Christian Yelich			J.D. Martinez
AVG.	.326		★ AVG.	.330
HR	36	ROUND 9	★ HR	43
RBI	110		★ RBI	130
RUNS	118 ★		RUNS	111
SB	22 ★		SB	6

CHRISTIAN YELICH

BOGMAN

These two couldn't have fit any better in their new homes, JD was 4th in MVP voting in the AL and Yelich won the NL MVP. There are really only 2 reasons this one is a debate, otherwise Yelich would win easily because while they are both great in 4 categories Yelich has SBs by a large margin over JD Martinez. The first reason is reliability, not only was JD Martinez great last season but he has 38 HRs, 100 RBI, 85 runs and hit .300 or better in 3 of the last 4 seasons. Yelich hasn't been nearly as consistent, he didn't have double digit HRs until his 4th season in the bigs and has crossed a .300 batting average only twice in 6 seasons. The other is expected regression for Yelich, everyone and their mother expects the power to come down because he had 15 more HRs than his previous career high and he had the highest HR/FB rate in the bigs at 35%, JD Martinez was 2nd at 29.5%. Even with some power regression I'm going to go with Yelich, Miller Park seems to fit him perfectly, he was better in the 2nd half of the season and SBs are a more scarce stat than power. Yelich doesn't feel like the risk to me that he does to others, so give me the MVP 10-9.

J.D. MARTINEZ

THE WELSH

This is a true heavyweight battle. Yelich represents everything about my drafting philosophy during the first two rounds in 2019. If you are going to reach for stolen bases this year (and I mean reach, not overextending to a top-125 guy at pick 90), I'd rather do it with the chalk guys in the top 24 picks. Guys like Yelich, Lindor and Ramírez touched every category. That takes us to J.D. versus Yelich. They sit side by side on early ADPs with J.D. taking a slight edge. Only two players in 2018 had a 30-100-100 season while hitting .325 or better: J.D. and Yelich. So, the obvious argument becomes about the stolen bases. Yelich had 22, while JD swiped six. If you look at Steamer projections, you'll see a near 20% decline in forecasted for Yelich with around a 10% decrease for J.D. That type of decline would be a huge factor here because of how close they are overall. Let's take that out though for a minute. From a 5x5 standpoint, Martinez beat Yelich 3-2. Martinez also showed up as a top-five performer in four of the five categories (stolen bases obviously not being a big factor). He was first in runs batted in, second in dongs, second in average and fifth in runs. I would tell you that taking the hit in stolen bases early with similar production across other categories is a safe bet, but I can confidently tell you I can count on one hand the safe bets which reside in the first round. J.D. is on that hand, Yelich is not. Yelich sees a dip, and J.D. is the elite play in a 12th round 10-9 decision.

★ ★ ★ WINNER - J.D. MARTINEZ 10-9 ★ ★ ★

2019 | *Judges Scorecard*

JAKE CIELY	CLAY LINK	NATE GRIMM
MARTINEZ 10-9	MARTINEZ 10-9	MARTINEZ 10-9

Round 9: Christian Yelich vs J.D. Martinez

PAUL GOLDSCHMIDT **VS** GIANCARLO STANTON

	PAUL GOLDSCHMIDT		ROUND 10		GIANCARLO STANTON	
AVG.	.290	★			.266	AVG.
HR	33			★	38	HR
RBI	83			★	100	RBI
RUNS	95			★	102	RUNS
SB	7	★			5	SB

PAUL GOLDSCHMIDT

THE WELSH

And everybody hurts... sometimes. Alright, he's no longer a D-back, and it still sucks. Get over it! Prior to Arizona installing the humidor, Goldschmidt consistently enjoyed averaging 100 run & 100 RBI seasons (2016 he had 95 RBI's) with roughly 30 bombs. The 2018 season saw him maintain his batting average and home run totals, but we saw a decline on the other 5x5 categories. Could a move out of Arizona actually be the best thing? Looking at his Home/Road splits it was almost night and day (Home average: .238 & Road average: .339). Home bombs totaled 12, while he launched 21 away from Chase Field. The Goldy of Old was consistently in top-five pick territory. He might be back. The stolen base numbers could play a big key here. St. Louis is not very aggressive on the bases. In 2017, Arizona was 14th on stolen bases per game, while St. Louis was 25th. Interestingly though, St. Louis averaged more stolen bases on the road than Arizona. Goldy should help this number adjust. Goldy isn't going to going to beat Stanton in home runs, but runs batted in and runs are certainly in play. Goldy has hit for .290 or better the last four years making average a lock. So, those stolen base numbers play a solid role in his value over the elite power totals Stanton produces. Steamer projects 11 steals for Goldschmidt in 2019. I am all-in on the return of Goldy in 2019. Also factoring in an overall drop in elite fantasy first baseman, I am firmly in the corner of "Team Goldschmidt." I expect a 10-7 decision in favor of the new Cardinals' first baseman.

GIANCARLO STANTON

BOGMAN

I would love to use this entire section to bitch and moan about the Goldschmidt trade, but he's gone! It's over, and he's not coming back! The Welsh and I differ on the significance of Goldy moving to St. Louis. I think it's a lateral move; whereas, he believes it's a positive move. I think that Pollock, Peralta and Escobar compare pretty well to Carpenter, DeJong and Ozuna, but we'll see how that works out. I think we can all agree the lineup around Stanton in New York is better than either Arizona or St. Louis. Runs batted in and runs scored are going to be close but shaded towards Stanton. Goldy will win the batting average category, but this really comes down to the potential for high end home runs for Stanton and steals for Goldy. Stanton has had as many as 59 bombs in a season (2017) when he won the MVP. Goldy has had as many as 32 stolen bases in 2016 when Chip Hale was the manager of the Diamondbacks. I believe the potential for Stanton's home runs is better than steals for Goldy because Stanton was adjusting to a new array of pitchers moving to the AL and will have more experience against a lot of those pitchers this year. When Mike Shildt took over at manger for the Cardinals, they were nineteenth in stolen base attempts (the Dbacks were tenth in that time). So, I just don't see the opportunity for many more swipes for Goldy. Give me the upside power potential for Stanton. These two heavyweights trade earthshaking blows, but in the end, Stanton will emerge victorious!

★ ★ ★ WINNER - PAUL GOLDSCHMIDT 10-8 ★ ★ ★

20 19

Judges Scorecard

PAUL SPORER	DEREK VAN RIPER	RYAN BLOOMFIELD
GOLDY 10-8	STANTON 10-9	GOLDY 10-7

Round 10: Paul Goldschmidt vs Giancarlo Stanton

JACOB DEGROM VS COREY KLUBER

	JACOB DEGROM		ROUND 11	COREY KLUBER	
WINS	10			WINS	20 ★
ERA	1.70 ★			ERA	2.89
WHIP	0.912 ★			WHIP	0.991
K	269 ★			K	222
IP	217.0 ★			IP	215.0

JACOB DEGROM

THE WELSH

The 2018 version of Jacob DeGrom was pure and utter dominance. His first and second half ERA splits both under 2.00. His home/road splits were almost mirror images of his first and second half ERA. He took the ERA title, all the strikeouts, and a Cy Young award. The only thing to pick apart are the win totals, but don't think DeGrom didn't do everything in his power to get those wins. How many of DeGrom's 32 starts do you think he gave up four or more earned runs? One! Just one! 31 starts of three runs or less! How many were one run or less? 21... Dominance! The Mets offensive support was an embarrassment, something they have aggressively tackled during the 2018 offseason. On the other hand, Kluber is coming off a huge 20-win season, his career high. Not many pitchers have been more consistent over the last five years than "Klu-Bot." 200 plus innings and 200+ strikeouts over the last five years. It's hard to say we are on a decline of any sort with Kluber, but we did see his strikeout percentage touch its lowest point in those five years (tying 2016 of 26.4%). We also saw a very soft decline in velocity of half a MPH. Neither of those things are a calling card for a down Kluber year, but we are talking about a different tier of pitcher at this point. Kluber's 5x5 category win over DeGrom was Wins, and during 2019, this gap should close. Take a clear-cut win in the other four categories, and DeGrom wins this in third round knockout.

COREY KLUBER

BOGMAN

Well, deGrom was better in almost everything in 2019. So, this one is a bit difficult to argue. deGrom won the Cy Young, was first in ERA, third in WHIP, and fourth in Ks, but he only could muster 10 wins with the pathetic offense around him. I understand and am with the crowd who doesn't like the wins category. If we switched it to quality starts, there would be no argument because it would be another category in which Jacob deGrom lead the league. Just like with stolen bases for hitters, wins for starters are the hardest stat to come by and as a result are the most notable stat for these two guys. Kluber doubled up deGrom 20 wins to 10. So, the question between these guys is, "Are the small differences in the ERA, WHIP, and strikeouts worth the difference in Wins?' Sure, we can expect Kluber probably won't win as many as 20 games and deGrom probably won't win as few as 10, but the difference in ERA will probably close as well. You may be right. I may be crazy, but I'll take the likelihood of the wins over small difference in ERA. I can make up the Ks later in draft as well. These two trade power punches and go the distance with Kluber edging out deGrom in a well fought bout.

★ ★ ★ WINNER - JACOB DEGROM 10-7 ★ ★ ★

2019 | Judges Scorecard

IN THIS LEAGUE

NICK POLLACK	JOE PISAPIA	KC BUBBA
DEGROM KO	DEGROM 10-9	DEGROM 10-8

Round 11: Jacob deGrom vs Corey Kluber

TREA TURNER vs MANNY MACHADO

	TREA TURNER		ROUND 12		MANNY MACHADO
AVG.	.271			★ AVG.	.297
HR	19			★ HR	37
RBI	73			★ RBI	107
RUNS	103 ★			RUNS	84
SB	43 ★			SB	14

TREA TURNER
THE WELSH

We're starting to move into a space where chasing stolen bases has become less desirable. The one trick ponies (a la Juan Pierre) aren't going to go in the top 40 or 50 picks anymore. You'll without a doubt find cheap stolen bases. There are a handful of players, however, in the top 20 to 25 picks who present such a solid mixture of 5x5 categories while giving you a huge jump on stolen bases (more than even I am comfortable letting this be your "reach for stolen bases" rather than "spreading it out"). Trea Turner is the perfect example. He is far from a one trick pony. Of those who finished in the top 10 in stolen bases in 2018, only two players had more RBI's than Turner: José Ramírez and Mookie Betts. In that same grouping, only two had more runs: Ramirez and Betts again. Factor in home runs, and we can add Starling Marte to Ramírez and Betts with the few who surpassed Turner. I am not so much as arguing that Turner is fantasy-wise better than Machado, but rather Turner is better for the construction of your team than Machado. Steamer projects these two with an almost identical batting average. So, this comes down to the power stats for Machado versus runs and steals for Turner. The difference in runs in favor of one corner is comparable to the difference in runs batting in for the other. Machado combined for 51 HR/SB, while Turner combined for 62 HR/SB. With Turner, I don't have to make up 25 HR's and 60 RBI's like I did a few years ago with Billy Hamilton. No more one trick ponies... just thoroughbreds! Turner in a last round KO.

MANNY MACHADO
BOGMAN

Trea Turner steals a lot of bases, and stolen bases are indeed scarce. It's hard to argue against drafting him because of it. The Nationals lineup is changing a bit this season though, and with it appears as if Trea Turner will be dropping to the two-hole in the batting order. He actually hit second more times than he did leadoff last season (329 at bats batting second versus 270 leading off), but his rate of stolen bases was much lower there. A full season at leadoff would have looked more like 56 steals with 35 swipes for a full season batting second. So, there is a dramatic drop off if he hits second most of the season. We also don't know for sure what kind of gap there will be between Turner and Machado in steals because Machado has stolen between twenty and zero in the last four years. The only inconsistent category in Machado's repertoire is steals. He's had at least 81 runs, 33 homers, and 86 driven in over the last four years while hitting .286 or better in three of those four years. You are buying consistency in drafting Manny Machado and buying steals and runs by selecting Trea Turner. In most cases, I'm going to lean towards consistency when I'm selecting players considering how early these two come off the board. Machado gets points deducted early in this bout for sneaking in a rabbit punch, but ends up earning the victory with a KO in the eight.

★ ★ ★ WINNER - TREA TURNER 10-7 ★ ★ ★

2019

Judges Scorecard

ROB SILVER	EDDY ALMAGUER	SAMMY REID
TURNER 10-7	TURNER 10-8	TURNER KO

Round 12: Trea Turner vs Manny Machado

OZZIE ALBIES VS CARLOS CORREA

AVG.	.261 ★		AVG.	.239
HR	24 ★	**ROUND 13**	HR	15
RBI	72 ★		RBI	65
RUNS	105 ★		RUNS	60
SB	14 ★		SB	3

OZZIE ALBIES

BOGMAN

I was actually really surprised by my thoughts on this debate when looking a little deeper. I knew that Albies had a bad second half after EXPLODING onto the scene. Ozzie only hit four home runs in the second half after hitting twenty in the first half. His batting average dropped 55 points from .281 to .226. Then, I couldn't believe when I looked at Carlos Correa, and his second half was actually worse than Albies. Correa hit .180 in the second half and only had two bombs. Carlos Correa probably still has a higher ceiling than Albies, but over the last two seasons, he has missed over 50 games in each season. Correa suffered a UCL sprain in 2017, and last year, he had turf toe, plantar fasciitis, an oblique strain, and a back sprain. It's clear I'm no doctor, but the chances of one of these cropping up again or a new soft tissue injury happening are fairly high. Ozzie Albies played in 158 games (a number Correa has yet to hit in his career), and now understands how to handle a full season in "The Bigs." Give me the guy who isn't injury prone. I know that Albies struggled in the second half of 2018, but the future is bright. More importantly, he doesn't have the injury history that Carlos Correa does. Correa's nagging injuries keep him from going the distance as Albies wins this bout!

CARLOS CORREA

THE WELSH

2018 was Correa's worst year to date. He only played 110 games and struggled with both his plate discipline and making good contact. Correa has a career .288/.273 left/right batting average split. In 2018, he maintained that average against lefties but dropped to a .223 against righties. He's been dead even for home/road splits with a career .277 and almost even numbers across the board, but again last year, he dropped to a .195 home average. There were few redeeming factors for Carlos Correa in 2018. There is one negative which could actually be spun a positive. As I mentioned, his plate discipline declined and did so at every single level! He swung at 2% more pitches outside the zone and 2% less inside the zone. His contact numbers broke even around the same percentage. He had just about an overall 3% dip in making contact. He simply never recovered from the constant barrage of injuries last year. What is positive about that? Simply put, it's a new year of health and a pinpointed area of focus: plate discipline. Still only 24 years young, Correa had been a perennial 20+ Home Run and .275 average middle of the order cornerstone. Now, let's take a peek at Albies. Though he had a very nice season, one which Correa has done before in his sleep, Albies had a horrid second half of 2018 posting a .228 average during the that timeframe with a final month which saw a .198 batting average. Last, this debate on the surface was about value. Correa is the big name. Albies is the up and comer. Looking at early NFBC average draft positions, these guys are both in the forties range typically within five picks of each other. I think during most drafts in March, you'll see Correa picked roughly ten to twenty spots before of Albies, which won't scare me away. I think Correa bounces back from the down year with a career high in homers and runs driven in. Albies has a fine season but ultimately struggles to match last year's numbers. Correa with a third-round knockdown. Albies gets up, last another three rounds before the fight is called.

★ ★ ★ WINNER - OZZIE ALBIES 10-9 ★ ★ ★

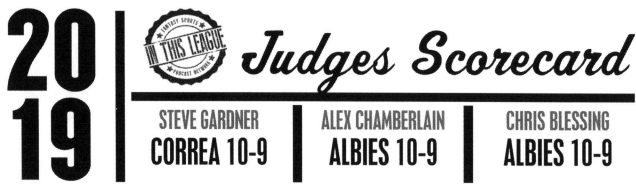

20 19

Judges Scorecard

STEVE GARDNER	ALEX CHAMBERLAIN	CHRIS BLESSING
CORREA 10-9	**ALBIES 10-9**	**ALBIES 10-9**

TREVOR BAUER VS NOAH SYNDERGAARD

	TREVOR BAUER		ROUND	NOAH SYNDERGAARD	
WINS	12			★ WINS	13
ERA	2.21 ★		14	ERA	3.03
WHIP	1.089 ★			WHIP	1.212
K	221 ★			K	155
IP	175.1 ★			IP	154.1

TREVOR BAUER
THE WELSH

I've notably never been a Trevor Bauer fan. His antics, crying, and blaming of teammates is quite tiresome. His 69/420 stuff was somewhat funny, and he is sometimes an inspiration with his donating campaigns. His refusal to sign a contract extension of more than one year due to a personal bet and his use of the fractions 69 and 420 is comparable the moment your parents starting using Facebook draining all of the fun out of it. In 2018, he was able to lessen the sound of the less redeeming personal traits with a dominant performance. Statistically, you can see how Bauer has been trending here. He has had an average around three free passes per nine innings while increasing his strikeouts per nine innings. Most notably, he had the league's lowest home run to fly ball percentage at 6.2%, the lowest since 2015 when Gio Gonzalez had a 5.9%. The biggest difference we can see in his deep arsenal is the use of both his cutter and slider in the same season with his slider being the higher usage pitch. Commonly, the slider and cutter can be seen as a similar pitch, but he knows how to vary the speed. He threw the slider about 10% more in 2018 than in 2017. Syndergaard's fantasy outlook is dreamy, but he's been somewhat of a nightmare recently. Injuries have hurt him as he saw a sharp decline last year in strikeouts. Thor is a fantasy pitcher we dream about but has disappointed as of late. Bauer matches Syndergaard's output with less injury risk. The floor may be higher for Bauer with similar ceiling. Bauer and Syndergaard "duke" it out, but 420 seconds into the match, Bauer knocks Syndergaard down with his 69th hook. Bauer wins!

NOAH SYNDERGAARD
BOGMAN

These guys both had weird years. For Trevor Bauer, he was on his way to a breakout season. Bauer had 175 strikeouts before fracturing his fibula and only pitching 39 innings in the second half. He snuck in nine and one-third innings before the playoffs, during which he pitched only four innings. Syndergaard on the other hand was coming back from his weird abdominal injury the Mets mishandled in 2017. Last season, he missed games with a finger injury and then with hand, foot and mouth disease. These guys are very similar. Their xFIP is close. Bauer took the K/9, while Syndergaard took the BB/9. The swinging strike rate was almost identical. This one might be the most razor thin of decisions so far, but I really like the way Thor ended the season with the Mets. Syndergaard gave up only seven runs in his last five starts, which included three games he didn't give up a run, and he capped 2018 off with a complete game shutout! Likeability should really have nothing to do in these debates, but it's also difficult for me to draft guys I don't want to root for. Syndergaard knocks out Bauer while he is preoccupied posting pictures on his Instagram account.

★ ★ ★ WINNER - NOAH SYNDERGAARD 10-9 ★ ★ ★

20 19 | IN THIS LEAGUE — FANTASY SPORTS PODCAST NETWORK — Judges Scorecard

JASON COLLETTE	NATE GRIMM	MATT MODICA
BAUER 10-8	THOR 10-9	THOR 10-9

Round 14: Trevor Bauer vs Noah Syndergaard

TREVOR STORY VS JAVIER BAEZ

	STORY		ROUND 15		BAEZ
AVG.	.291	★			AVG.	.290
HR	37	★			HR	34
RBI	108			★	RBI	111
RUNS	88			★	RUNS	101
SB	27	★			SB	21

TREVOR STORY

BOGMAN

The stats were crazy similar for these two in 2018! Also, they both play shortstop. Even their birthdays are only separated by two weeks! They both seemed to reach their potential last season finishing with over 30 home runs, 20 swipes and hitting over .290. I think it's tough to realistically expect these numbers again. So, I want to choose the guy who is least likely to regress. The splits are almost identical. As expected, Story hits better at Coors. Unexpectedly, Báez hits better away from Wrigley. They BOTH hit .292 before the break and .289 after. We need to look at some of the underlying numbers, and those lean towards Story in a big way. Story owns Báez in Swinging Strike Percentage (SwStr%) (11.4%-17.9%), BB% (7.2%-4.5%) and OBP (.348-.326). Story also had a way more realistic HR/FB ratio at 19.9% (career 19.6%) compared to Baez's 24.3% (career 18.6%). Story had a much better Hard Contact rate at 44.5 % (career 43.2%) than Báez at 35.8% (career 32.7%). Story has the better underlying numbers and hits in the better park. I'll lean on him in this one. Story's sabermetrics help him to edge out Báez in a majority decision.

JAVIER BÁEZ

THE WELSH

Well, looky here! This debate is back for a second straight year! We covered this in the 2018 review pages. Unlike some of the reviews, this one was argued by both Bogman and I, and we were both right! Both players no reside in the second-round range of value with Báez getting an edge over Story per early NFBC average draft positions. Story's tale was all about contact. He made huge strides jumping 7% in overall contact producing an even 7% contact boost both inside and outside of the strike zone. He even pulled the ball 5% more while bumping his hard-hit contact by 4%. I'm not making the case for Story though. This is all about Bae(z). I do wonder if some of those dramatic changes are all sustainable for Story. Elite players make adjustments, but when it's as dramatic as Story's 2018 campaign, it can cause us to press pause and take a deeper look. Báez has consistently been trending in this direction. He was a top ten in HR/FB in 2018. He made some nice, gradual jumps in contact like Story, rising his contact inside the zone by more than 4%. Ok, so let's recap. Story had a meteoric rise. Báez made subtle adjustments to continue his trend. His most important takeaway from 2018 was his move to a full-time player, yet they both got to the same spot. The issue at hand is a massive jump in price tag for both players. You have to come to terms with who can maintain this production. I say, "Báez" as the "story" was leading to this spot. Only three players in 2018 had a .300 20-100-100-30 season, can you guess who? Ramírez is one. Yelich is two. And of course, Báez is three. Maybe one gets knocked out this year, after being an underdog match in 2018, but Báez wins 10-8 by decision.

★ ★ ★ **WINNER - JAVIER BÁEZ 10-9** ★ ★ ★

2019

IN THIS LEAGUE · *Judges Scorecard*

JOE PISAPIA	JAKE CIELY	ITL ARMY
STORY 10-9	**BÁEZ 10-9**	**BÁEZ 10-8** (67%)

Round 15: Trevor Story vs Javier Báez

AARON JUDGE VS KHRIS DAVIS

	AARON JUDGE			KHRIS DAVIS	
AVG.	.278 ★		AVG.		.247
HR	27		★ HR		48
RBI	67		★ RBI		123
RUNS	77		★ RUNS		98
SB	6 ★		SB		0

ROUND 16

AARON JUDGE

THE WELSH

Value debates are where it's at. Judge the obvious pick here; you're not taking Davis over him, but the question is, is Davis' 3-4 round draft spot a better pick than a second round Judge? I've never seen a player more consistent than Khris Davis. It's almost weird. He's produced four straight .247 average seasons. When's the last time someone had the exact same average for four straight years? Upside, though? You have to admit, as nice as it is, you know what you're getting, you aren't playing for any upside. He will hurt your average without question, which is not ideal in OBP leagues. Everyone called for the "Judge decline" in 2018. It happened to a degree, but injuries were the underlying reason. His power numbers from 2017 were nutty; .350 ISO and an unsustainable 35%+ HR/FB. He just came down to earth a little in 2018 with a .249 ISO and a 29% HR/FB ratio, which would have been third if he qualified. Projections want judge to hit .250, yet he has hit .284 and .279 the last two years. His walk percentage is also in the teens for you OBP'ers. Projections are tempered on Judge this year, but a .270-40-100-100 season is very much within reach. Now, are those numbers worth a two round boost over Davis, who essentially just hits for a lower average? They are, because I gave you reasonable numbers for a full Judge season. That isn't the ceiling. 2017's .284-52-128-114 is a ceiling - Something Khris Davis will not touch. That risk vs. reward is well worth the two round swing. Judge's verdict: 2nd round knockout, case dismissed.

KHRIS DAVIS

BOGMAN

If we're arguing this one straight up, it's challenging to recommend taking Davis over Judge. Judge is in the better lineup, a much more hitter friendly park, and offers more upside than Khris Davis. Luckily, you can get Davis two rounds after Judge is drafted. So, not only can you take Davis in this situation, but you can also get another great player in the second round where you could have selected Judge! Judge is likely to win batting average since Khris Davis has hit .247 literally in four straight seasons. One can presume Judge can also take steals, but he has never had more than nine. So, it won't be by a lot. The big thing here is the power categories in R, HR and RBI which is why we draft either one of these guys. Judge has played only 2 full seasons and has had struggles in the 2nd half of both, the first one his averaged plunged to .228 in the 2nd half because of a shoulder injury and last season he only played 18 games post break because of a wrist injury. Khris Davis might be boring but he's boring to the tune on 150 games played, 42 HRs, 102 RBI and 85 runs scored as his lows the last 3 seasons. I honestly think this is a fairly easy debate when considering the pairing you can make taking Davis 2 rounds later.

★ ★ ★ **WINNER - KHRIS DAVIS 10-9** ★ ★ ★

20 19

Judges Scorecard

IN THIS LEAGUE

EDDY ALMAGUER
DAVIS 10-8

PAUL SPORER
JUDGE KO

RYAN BLOOMFIELD
DAVIS 10-8

Round 16: Aaron Judge vs Khris Davis

FREDDIE FREEMAN VS VLADIMIR GUERRERO JR.

AVG.	.309			AVG.	.381
HR	23 ★	**ROUND 17**	★	HR	20
RBI	98 ★			RBI	78
RUNS	94 ★			RUNS	67
SB	10 ★			SB	3

*2018 MiLB Stats

FREDDIE FREEMAN

BOGMAN

It is not crazy Vladimir Guerrero Jr. is already being drafted in the top 40. He probably should have gotten an opportunity to come up last season for the Blue Jays as he has torn apart every level of Minor League Baseball in which he has played. The 19-year-old is the definition of a phenom: amazing bat speed, as much raw power as any prospect, and the impeccable bloodline. I have very little doubt that Vlad will be a major league success from the jump, but the fact remains he has yet to see MLB pitching. I know people just scoffed at this fact, but it's not just about the first go through against top level pitching. It's the second time those pitchers get a look at him and the third go-around. He must face the Red Sox, Yankees and Rays rotations, which is a tall task for anyone. Vlad will also be adjusting to a new country in Canada (eh!), the longest season he has ever encountered, and a laborious travel schedule. Adjusting to everything at once can be daunting, even for the top rookie. So instead of taking a risk on Vlad, why not take a "Steady Eddie" like Freddie Freeman? Freeman is all but guaranteed to produce a .300 batting average with 90 runs scored, 90 driven in, and approximately 25 homers. He even chipped in with ten swipes last year. It's an easy decision to go with Freeman, even if it's a round earlier than Vlad, and wait to take a risk somewhere later in the draft. Freeman disposes of the journeyman in a unanimous decision.

VLADIMIR GUERRERO JR.

THE WELSH

Here we are. 2019, the year of Vladimir Guerrero Jr., or as my son calls him, Bladdy (V's go by the wayside when you're six years old). I know this one makes you scratch your head, but this is 2019, and Vladimir Guerrero Jr. is going to go in your redraft league way higher than you might be ready for. Early drafts at First Pitch Arizona saw Vladdy going inside the top 20. Early NFBC ADP's in January have Vlad inside the top 40. You're going to have to understand, he will cost somewhere between a 20 and 30 overall pick in most leagues. Speaking of First Pitch, my favorite moment was sitting with some of the industries best fantasy minds at Scottsdale Stadium. Jason Collette sits down with the group and says, "steamer projections our out, guess who they have with the league's best average?" The entire group of degenerates that we are, in unison said "Vladimir Guerrero Jr!" That's right, the guy that hasn't played an inning of baseball at the major league level is Steamer's highest projection for average in the 2019 season. I watched Vladimir up close and personal during the Arizona Fall League, and no secret, he's something special. He doesn't strikeout, he finds his pitch, makes solid contact almost every time, and is going to be a force in the MLB even at 20. It's a lofty task to take a chalk player like Freddie Freeman and pass him at this cost, for an unproven talent. Last year we did it with Acuna, but not at a top three round cost. Projections have these two, amazingly very similar. Give the edge on RBI/RUNS to Freeman, and the AVG to Vlad Jr. If there was ever a year to take a risk on unproven major league talent, this is the year with Vladimir Guerrero Jr. Vlad Jr. with a 10-9 decision.

★ ★ ★ **WINNER - FREDDIE FREEMAN 10-8** ★ ★ ★

Judges Scorecard

2019

ROB SILVER	JAMES ANDERSON	CLAY LINK
FREEMAN 10-8	FREEMAN 10-8	FREEMAN 10-9

Round 17: Freddie Freeman vs Vladimir Guerrero Jr.

GERRIT COLE ⸻ VS ⸻ JUSTIN VERLANDER

	COLE			VERLANDER
WINS	15		★ WINS	16
ERA	2.88	ROUND	★ ERA	2.52
WHIP	1.033	18	★ WHIP	0.902
K	276		★ K	290
IP	200.1		★ IP	214.0

GERRIT COLE

THE WELSH

These two were like mirror images of each other, albeit one was seven years younger. They both went over 200 innings and pitched with over 250 strikeouts each. Mid two ERA's, middle teens on wins. The biggest difference was how Cole found himself in Houston. The pieces came together, if you will. His biggest changes came from some minimal boosts in FB and SLD velocity (career high 96.6 FB avg velocity), but the biggest was his drop in use of the changeup, down to 4.5%, while upping his curveball usage to a career high 19.3%. It greatly mirrors Justin Verlander's mix of pitches. Only seven players had a swinging strike percentage of 14 or greater. Cole and Verlander were seven and six on that list. For Verlander, it could be age finally creeping in. He'll be 36 this coming year. It seems like 35 is when we begin to use the phrase "don't catch a falling knife." Let's talk about value, or even perceived value. Verlander will go in front of Cole. ADP's show within 12 picks of each other, but most likely drafted in a different round. Give me the younger, cheaper 15+ win, 200+ strikeout Astros pitcher for 2019. Cole wins in a 10-8 decision.

JUSTIN VERLANDER

BOGMAN

Come on now, let's not get too cute here right? I LOVE Gerrit Cole and drafted him in a bunch of spots last season and it paid off! He had the 'breakout season' we have all been expecting at some point. Cole took his K/9 up to 12.4 and struck out 276 destroying his previous highs of 9.00 and 202. He also set career highs in Ws, WHIP and SwStr%. Justin Verlander set some career highs as well at the ripe old age of 35, in fact he ALSO set career highs in ERA, K/9, K, WHIP and SwStr% just like Cole. These two were even close in xFIP with Verlander at 3.03 and Cole at 3.04. The biggest stat separating these two is BB and BB/9, Verlander had the upper hand here only walking 37 last season with a BB/9 of 1.56 (career low) while Cole walked 64 with a BB/9 of 2.88 (both career highs). Pitching is so inconsistent from year to year that if you have a consistent performer they are almost always going to get the edge over the upside guy. While Verlander hasn't always been as good as he was in the 2018 season he has had 15 wins or more in 10 of his 13 seasons, ERA of 3.50 or lower in 9 seasons, 200+ Ks in 8 seasons and he's done all of those in 3 straight seasons. Cole is great but these guys are going within a few picks of each other so let's just stick with the proven guy at this point. 10-8 Verlander at the scorecard!

★ ★ ★ WINNER - JUSTIN VERLANDER 10-9 ★ ★ ★

20 19

Judges Scorecard

NICK POLLACK	ENO SARRIS	SAMMY REID
VERLANDER 10-9	COLE 10-9	VERLANDER 10-9

Round 18: Gerrit Cole vs Justin Verlander

CODY BELLINGER
vs
RHYS HOSKINS

ROUND 19

	CODY BELLINGER			RHYS HOSKINS
AVG.	.260 ★		AVG.	.246
HR	25		★ HR	34
RBI	76		★ RBI	96
RUNS	84		★ RUNS	89
SB	14 ★		SB	5

CODY BELLINGER

THE WELSH

Bellinger took a step back in 2018; partially due to the fact that his production had to come down to earth from his rookie season. This is kind of mixed in with the "sophomore slump" narrative. He had an ISO over .300 which wasn't going to last. He had a HR/FB rate which was 10th best in all of baseball in 2017. It dropped more than we wanted, which led to a HR decrease. He's more of a free swinger than Hoskins, which leaves him more prone to slumps. The two had very similar walk/strikeout rates in 2018, but Bellinger makes less contact in and out of zone, while swinging at those pitches more often. Bellingers "value" swings are higher or lower than Hoskins due to some of this volatility. With these two so similar, one thing that puts Bellinger over for me is how they both finished their 2018 season. Bellinger hit .285 in the second half, which was about 40 points higher than the first half, while Hoskins finished the 2nd half hitting .237, which was about 20 points lower than the first half. Adjustments are so key with these young free swinging power bats. Let's throw in the other important side bar, that Bellinger steals bases. He's had double digit steals in both of his pro seasons. Only three other first baseman stole double digit bases last year - Myers, Goldy and Rizzo. I think Bellinger will continue what he did in the second half of last year, allowing himself a 3 out of 5, 5x5 category win, and a 10-8 victory of Hoskins.

RHYS HOSKINS

BOGMAN

This one is pretty tough to argue one way or the other. Both are in their third season with nothing left to prove after last year. They both hit cleanup in good lineups and are both very streaky posting a month of under .200 and over .310 in 2018. I'm leaning towards Hoskins in this debate for a few reasons. First, one must take in account the improvement in the Phillies lineup. They added Jean Segura and Andrew McCutchen thus far and have been openly stating they are willing to outspend other teams for current free agents. Going into the season, they are a team that can deal from the depth of their minor league system to add more to their MLB lineup. Second, Bellinger weirdly dropped off four of the five standard categories during his second season while playing MORE games last year. Next, Hoskins smoked Bellinger in Contact%: 79.8% (54th in "The Bigs") for Rhys and 72.5% (125th) for Bellinger. I know that Bellinger has the stolen bases edge over Hoskins, and it is the reason he might go higher in your draft. I fear the bottom dropping out from Bellinger much more than from Hoskins, resulting in me avoiding Bellinger. Hoskins and Bellinger trade blows, but similar to their hitting contact percentage, Hoskins lands the majority of his punches and emerges victorious in a split decision.

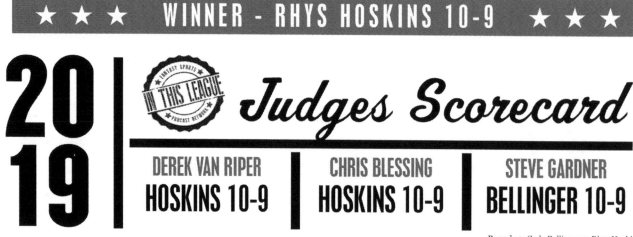

★ ★ ★ WINNER - RHYS HOSKINS 10-9 ★ ★ ★

20 19

Judges Scorecard

IN THIS LEAGUE · FANTASY SPORTS · PODCAST NETWORK

DEREK VAN RIPER	CHRIS BLESSING	STEVE GARDNER
HOSKINS 10-9	HOSKINS 10-9	BELLINGER 10-9

Round 19: Cody Bellinger vs Rhys Hoskins

GEORGE SPRINGER **VS** JUAN SOTO

	GEORGE SPRINGER		ROUND 20		JUAN SOTO	
AVG.	.265			★	AVG.	.292
HR	22				HR	22
RBI	71	★			RBI	70
RUNS	102	★			RUNS	77
SB	6	★			SB	5

GEORGE SPRINGER

THE WELSH

What Juan Soto did at his age in 2018 in the major leagues, was a story legends carry around. No one expected him to come up, and not only did he do so, he dominated at the same level he did in the minors. Can Soto repeat it? That's the big question. He makes the right decisions and makes the right contact to suggest that a lot of it is possible. The issue though, is that he comes at a top 30 price for 2019. He essentially replaced the old spot that Springer filled. A potential .280-30-100-90 and 20+ stolen bases (if the Astros would just let him run), has always had fantasy owners targeting him. Springer's 2018 wasn't great, and saw some career lows in home runs, runs and RBI's when he puts in an almost full season. The funny thing is outside of a little increase in out of the zone swinging, and decrease on inside the zone swinging, Springer repeated a lot of the things that made his 2017 so great. Springer also finished 2018 on a high note hitting .301 from his .253 first half, which I think signals to the lower numbers being more fluke than fact. Springer hit mainly out of the leadoff spot, which will mute the RBI numbers, and the Astros just don't run him which keeps his overall potential at bay, but his ADP is what swings this debate. Soto is going in the 25-35 range. Springer, though, is going between 50-60. Unless it's an OBP league, Soto will not justify going multi rounds above Springer. King George takes down Childish Bambino with a 10th round KO.

JUAN SOTO

BOGMAN

These guys were almost a mirror image of each other in 2018. The big differences being in batting average with Soto smashing in that .292-.265 and Springer winning in Runs by 25 at 102-77. They were tied in HRs, Springer got him by 1 in RBI and SBs all while Soto played 24 fewer games than Springer. We can assume that Soto is going to come down a little bit from his amazing rookie performance but most of the advanced stats are in his favor as well. Soto has the lower SwStr%, his BABIP was lower, BB% higher, made more Hard Contact, less Soft Contact and more contact overall! The only thing that Springer really has going for him in this matchup is that he is going to hit leadoff so he could have more SB opportunities but with the Astros great lineup they have been taking fewer chances on the basepaths, while the Nationals were a top 5 team in SBs last season. You can get Springer about 2 and a half rounds after Soto is going but with the arrow pointing up for Juan I don't know that this is a 'get most of his production' type of return. Soto first round KO!

WINNER - JUAN SOTO 10-8

2019

Judges Scorecard

IN THIS LEAGUE — FANTASY SPORTS — PODCAST NETWORK

JAMES ANDERSON
SOTO KO

JAKE CIELY
SPRINGER 10-9

JASON COLLETTE
SOTO 10-9

Round 20: George Springer vs Juan Soto

STARLING MARTÉ VS CHARLIE BLACKMON

	STARLING MARTE				CHARLIE BLACKMON	
AVG.	.277			★ AVG.	.291
HR	20		ROUND	★ HR	29
RBI	72 ★		21	RBI	70
RUNS	81			★ RUNS	119
SB	33 ★			SB	12

STARLING MARTÉ

BOGMAN

Both guys had "down" seasons by their standards. Blackmon was a first round pick last season, and while his production was great, he declined in each category in comparison to 2017. Marté was good, but he sustained three separate injuries last year: one to his oblique, he took a 95 MPH pitch off his hand, and he strained his calf late in the season. This is an easy debate because you can a good amount of production in the other categories, and Marté should dominate in steals. Blackmon has historically had more complete five category seasons, but he's evolved into more of a power hitter over the last three seasons with the speed taking a back seat. Marté swiped 25 bases last season in the first half alone. He slowed to only eight during the second half due to being in Clint Hurdle's dog house and the multitude of injuries. Blackmon has lowered his stolen base total and attempt rate over the last four years. At this rate, he won't hit double digits this season. Marté is also going just almost a full round behind Blackmon in drafts this year. So, you can pair an elite pitcher with Marté and pick up power later in the draft. Marté's combinations are too fast for Blackmon to counterpunch as Chuck Nazty loses to the righty.

CHARLIE BLACKMON

THE WELSH

Boy has Charlie Blackmon been good. It's also so amazing to see what happens to great players when they "underperform" on their expectations. Blackmon was a top 5 pick in 2018, and now locked into the third round. Over the last three years, Blackmon has averaged 31 HR's, 122 RUN's, 85 RBI's, 14 SB's and a .315 average. That's a full "stuff and things" 5x5 stud. His dip in 2018 affected his RBI's and AVG. Another positive sign, he raised his AVG in the second half by ten points, hitting just under .300. Think of the discounts you're getting on guys that were studs who massively underperformed last year, and think of the discount you are getting on Blackmon for little to no reason. His underlying stats show he pressed a little and needs to get the ball back in the air a bit more. I'll take the bet that he does it all day, every day. Marté is no slouch himself, he was in an exclusive group of one of only three to hit 20 HR's and steal 30 bases. My issue when comparing the two is his average RUN and lower than average RBI totals. He's an above average hitter, but still probably has a 20 point difference with Blackmon. Take into account Marté was caught being a dirty cheater; Blackmon is the type of safe player with high production that allows you to take some chances in other sports (ala Vladimir Guerrero Jr.). Charlie BLACKmon with a 1st round KO. BLACKMON WINS, BLACKMON WINS!

★ ★ ★ WINNER - CHARLIE BLACKMON 10-9 ★ ★ ★

20 19

Judges Scorecard

PAUL SPORER	JOE PISAPIA	ROB SILVER
BLACKMON 10-9	**MARTÉ 10-9**	**BLACKMON 10-9**

Round 21: Starling Marté vs Charlie Blackmon

ANTHONY RIZZO VS JOEY VOTTO

				ROUND			AVG.	.284

ANTHONY RIZZO

AVG. .283
HR 25 ★
RBI 101 ★
RUNS 74 ★
SB 6 ★

ROUND 22

★ AVG. .284
HR 12
RBI 67
RUNS 67
SB 2

ANTHONY RIZZO
THE WELSH

This used to be the elite of elite first base debates. Votto has some similarities in 2018 to his down 2014 season. Ultimately, we could look at this and say, he can make some of the similar adjustments from before, and have a major bounce back, especially considering his ADP. We could also look at his age, and ask how much have the odds decreased that he makes a full bounce back at almost 35. I think it's somewhere between the two extremes. He's not Votto of old, but not the Votto we've known. Rizzo had a split year. The first half was incredibly forgettable, while he ended the second half hitting .324. It wasn't a "down" year per say, but more of a "come back to reality" year. His home run and run totals took a hit, while the promising prospects of stolen bases diminished. What's interesting between these two, is how Votto has been known to be so patient and selective that he hurts himself. He swung at only 39.7% of pitches. That was tied for 15th lowest among qualified MLB batters. On the other end, Rizzo was almost too aggressive last year. His 47.4% swing rate isn't the issue, but he had a 3% rise in swing % inside the zone, and a 2% increase in contact %. Why is that bad? Usually it's not, but he had a rise in line drive % and medium hit %. Top that with his HR/FB dropping 3%. What I'm saying is, even though he made more contact, it wasn't good contact. Amazingly, he dropped his strikeout percentage by a full percent, but that's because he was swinging at everything and making ok contact. All that nonsense right there, tells me Rizzo will be just fine. Even though Rizzo comes in at a very steep discount, it doesn't matter. Rizzo with a 2nd round KO.

JOEY VOTTO
BOGMAN

These guys have both dropped dramatically from where they were selected in last season's drafts, which makes sense for Votto but not really for Rizzo. Rizzo has dropped a full round in 12-team drafts from twenty-fourth to thirty-sixth. He slumped a little bit across four of five categories from 2017 to 2018, but with first basemen dropping so much as a group, it's surprising to see that big of a fall. Votto dropped 60 spots from sixteenth to seventy-sixth, which made a lot of sense with the awful year he had. Votto dropped in literally everything: .36 points in batting average, 39 fewer runs, 24 less homers, 33 driven in, and 3 less steals. I have to think this enormous drop in production was because of the injury plagued season he endured in 2018. Votto started off with a back injury in May followed by knee and leg injuries later in the season. Votto had an injury riddled 2014 season, where he only played 62 games, and it was the last time before 2018 he hit under .300. Votto then bounced back with three straight seasons of .310+, 95 R, 29 HR and 80+ RBI so the return to form has happened before. Rizzo is in the better of the two lineups and will probably put up better numbers. The cost for him is so much higher than Votto. I would rather take Votto because of the massive drop off in his ADP this year. There are still good players to draft around Votto, but they aren't the upper echelon players going around Rizzo. So, I think this bout is close, but a scorecard victory for Votto.

★ ★ ★ WINNER - ANTHONY RIZZO 10-8 ★ ★ ★

20 19 Judges Scorecard

IN THIS LEAGUE

ALEX CHAMBERLAIN	STEVE GARDNER	CLAY LINK
RIZZO 10-7	RIZZO 10-8	DRAW

Round 22: Anthony Rizzo vs Joey Votto

AARON NOLA VS LUIS SEVERINO

			ROUND 23		
WINS	17			★ WINS	19
ERA	2.37 ★			ERA	3.39
WHIP	0.975 ★			WHIP	1.145
K	224 ★			K	220
IP	212.1 ★			IP	191.1

AARON NOLA

BOGMAN

These guys are like the NL and AL versions of each other when analyzing their stat lines. Both had career high wins, more than 220 strikeouts, and a 12.4 SwStr%. Most of the differences were miniscule. Nola won in ERA, but Severino was better in xFIP. Nola won WHIP by a small margin, yet Severino had a slightly better BB/9. Nola had a better GB/FB rate, while Severino had a much more sustainable LOB%. I could go more in depth on the closeness of these stats, but needless to say, it gets to the point these guys are almost interchangeable. There are a few reasons why I'm more slightly on the Nola bandwagon instead of Severino. The first one is he has a lower fly ball rate than Severino. Both being in hitters' parks, I'll take the guy less likely to give up the long ball. Nola also induces more soft contact and less hard contact than Severino. This one may be a little bit more obvious, but Nola playing in the National League getting to face more pitchers/pinch hitters and less designated hitters should count for something. It's still a razor thin matchup but those small differences get me to lean in favor of Nola. Nola bests the Dominican in a split decision.

LUIS SEVERINO

THE WELSH

These two right here are the prime "I missed the elite options, oh crap, what do I do" picks. You don't get Scherzer or Sale, but you get two of the best young slingers in the game. One issue I have with both though, is their ADP. Both seemingly come at a bit too high of a cost. Aaron Nola's early ADP's show right at the top of the third, which I don't like. Here is an edge for Severino, as his is right around the start of the fourth. If you see them as relative equals, then this is a no brainer. The sign on Severino's back doesn't read kick me, it reads "second half." Severino was masterful in the first half, striking out 144 to Nola's 135, only walking 32 to Nola's 35, and having almost identical ERA's with .01 of each other. He just fell apart in the second half, finishing with a 5.57 ERA. Even with a horrid second half, Severino finished with more wins, a higher K/9 and a lower B/9. Take that into consideration with Severino's clear win over Nola in 2017. If I'm getting a full round discount on Severino, you've got your winner. Severino by 10-8 decision after 12.

★ ★ ★ WINNER - AARON NOLA 10-7 ★ ★ ★

20 19

Judges Scorecard

NICK POLLACK	DEREK VAN RIPER	SAMMY REID
NOLA KO	NOLA 10-8	NOLA 10-9

Round 23: Aaron Nola vs Luis Severino

COREY SEAGER VS GLEYBER TORRES

	COREY SEAGER		GLEYBER TORRES
AVG.	.267	★ AVG.	.271
HR	2	★ HR	24
RBI	13	★ RBI	77
RUNS	13	★ RUNS	54
SB	0	★ SB	6

ROUND 24

COREY SEAGER

THE WELSH

It's been two years since Corey Seager caught a break. One of the most talked about and promising shortstops, and then it came to a screeching halt after two injury plagued years. Currently, he is coming off of Tommy John surgery in August. Unlike with Pitchers, he's expected to be fully healthy and ready to go for spring training. So do you like to gamble? That's what you'll have to do here, at least early on. The earlier the draft, the later he will go. In January Seagers ADP is in the 80-90 range. As soon as he gets into spring training games (and presumably not held back the entire spring) his ADP will rise and rise. What then makes it tougher, is when Seager and Torres are near one another. Seager's most recent actual year in 2017, was essentially Torres' rookie year. That was a bit of a downer for Seager btw. Seager is a major force for runs and average, very solid on home runs and useful for RBI's. Gleyber shares many of the same traits, just replace runs with RBI's. This is where risk/reward comes into play. Seager can and will outperform Torres in 2019 if the games played are equal. I'll stupidly make this bet. The gamble is the games player. Taking current costs into consideration, Seager wins this one standing up. 4th round KO.

GLEYBER TORRES

BOGMAN

This is probably the easiest debate we have in my opinion. For some reason, it escapes me wholly and completely. People still think that Corey Seager is going to "breakout" smashing a million homers while winning a batting title because he performed very well in the minors. His home runs will end up in the mid-twenties range. Seager will put up solid run and RBI totals while having a batting average around .300. The one thing he does better than most of the shortstops who will start in your league is hit for average. He's coming off both Tommy John AND hip surgery. In fact, he had to hold off on having hip surgery until his arm was healthy enough for him to handle the crutches for his hip surgery. We truly should wonder how much the Dodgers are going to baby as he returns in 2019. Torres hit 24 round-trippers in only 123 games last season. It's not out of the realm of possibility he could get to 30 over 162 games. He'll qualify at shortstop in almost all formats after playing 21 games there last year. Gleyber's six stolen bases during last year are already two more than Seager has tallied in a single season. Gleyber has more power, qualifies at short and second, and isn't an injury risk. Easy choice. Seager's corner has to throw in the towel after being pummeled by Torres.

★ ★ ★ WINNER - COREY SEAGER 10-8 ★ ★ ★

2019

IN THIS LEAGUE *Judges Scorecard*

JAKE CIELY	EDDY ALMAGUER	NATE GRIMM
SEAGER 10-8	SEAGER 10-8	SEAGER 10-8

Round 24: Corey Seager vs Gleyber Torres

ADALBERTO MONDESI VS WHIT MERRIFIELD

	ADALBERTO MONDESI				WHIT MERRIFIELD
AVG.	.276		★ AVG.	.304
HR	14 ★		HR	12
RBI	37		★ RBI	60
RUNS	47		★ RUNS	88
SB	32		★ SB	45

ROUND 25

ADALBERTO MONDESI

BOGMAN

The hype for Mondesi is real! Everyone is talking about how we can't extrapolate what Mondesi did over less than half a season and of course that's true. I don't think anyone would expect him to hit 30 HRs and steal 70 bases. Mondesi has scary underlying numbers as well, starting with a miserable 18.2% SwStr which would be in the Joey Gallo range. Mondesi also had a high HR/FB at 19.7%, below average K% at 26.5% and his BB% was awful at 3.8%. Sometimes though we forget that the bottom line is the 5 stats that we actually count and that is why I like Mondesi this year. Mondesi is being drafted just about a full round behind Merrifield at this point and I believe he will finish better than him in at least 3 categories. Mondesi should finish with more HRs, SBs and RBI than Merrifield with the possibility of getting him in Runs also. The only category that I would guarantee for Whit is batting average in this debate, runs are probable because Whit is slated to hit leadoff with Mondesi hitting 2. The bottom out is the real fear for Mondesi, struggling to hit .200 early could see him lose playing time but, there is no one waiting in the wings to usurp him so he'll get a long leash and he improved down the stretch last season (.250 pre break and .286 post break). There isn't a compelling reason not to take Merrifield for me but if I'm deciding between the two give me Mond-esi with that upside edge!

WHIT MERRIFIELD

THE WELSH

No player comes into 2019 with more hype than Adalberto Mondesi. Here is my least technically backed argument for any debate. How on God's green earth can Mondesi live up to the hype? His insane end to 2018 has people waiting with open arms for 2019 for a 30 home run, 60 stolen base season. Bold call guys, that ain't happening. When I look at Steamer projections, even those are jaw dropping with a 20-70-70-40 range season (the .250 avg is not so jaw dropping). Now let's say Steamer is right, then we're talking about a fourth round evaluation. But you can get this season, with lower home runs, much better average and way less risk from his teammate Whit Merrifield. Whit swung a bit less, but in the vein of being a more disciplined hitter. He walked 4% more and raised his average 20 points. His selectivity caused a bit of a drop in his power numbers, but he became a premier fantasy asset, leading the majors in stolen bases. Whit has built his floor. His two year average of 15 home runs, 39 stolen bases and a .290 average we will take all day every day. Mondesi's floor has quite a wide range of outcomes. Last year, Mondesi had a 26.5% strikeout rate, to go with a .271 average. How many batters do you think struckout 26% or greater and had an average of .270 or higher in 2019? Zero. Here's a few guys in 2017 who had a 26% strikeout rate and hit .270 or better, Domingo Santana and Tim Beckham. That went well in 2018. The closest comparison to his skill set that maintains at a high level is Javier Baez. Low walk rate, high strikeout rate, punishes with contact. Is Mondesi more Baez or Beckham? You'll have to pay a 3rd or 4th round to find out. I think Mondesi can be very productive this year, but I'm betting the under on Steamer projections. Merrifield represents the already reached upside, and massive floor that you rarely see outside the second round. Merrifield with a 3rd round knockout.

★ ★ ★ **WINNER - WHIT MERRIFIELD 10-8** ★ ★ ★

2019

Judges Scorecard

PAUL SPORER	ENO SARRIS	JASON COLLETTE
MERRIFIELD 10-8	MONDESI 10-9	MERRIFIELD KO

Round 25: Adalberto Mondesi vs Whit Merrifield

KENLEY JANSEN

VS

CRAIG KIMBREL

	KENLEY JANSEN		ROUND		CRAIG KIMBREL	
	SAVES	38		★	SAVES	42
	ERA	3.01	**26**	★	ERA	2.74
	WHIP	0.991 ★			WHIP	0.995
	K	82		★	K	96
	IP	71.2 ★			IP	62.1

KENLEY JANSEN
THE WELSH

If there was ever a year where I would own Kenley Jansen, it's this year. Last year, the elite closer crowd priced the top guys way out of any reasonable range for my taste. This year, those closers as a whole have backed off a bit, and now Jansen may not even be one of the first two closers off the board. Jansen's 2018 was mired by health issues and an incredibly bad August which sent fantasy owners into a tailspin. Jansen's bad start to the season didn't help, but he had many dominante months, that allowed him to finish the 1st half with an ERA of 2.33, but the rough second half was just about two runs higher with a 4.26 ERA. The narrative for Jansen is very negative going into this year. That second half ERA and the destruction of many fantasy teams is a huge cloud for owners. In the off-season, he had corrective heart surgery. Regardless of the surgery, people will look at the health issues from last year, see "heart surgery" this year, and want to avoid. Some people are risk avert, I am not one. Luckily that surgery went great, and he's expected to be stronger than ever now that it is all behind him. We overlook things like Kimbrel having a worse half, ERA wise, than Jansen with a 4.57 ERA. Jansen had four out of the six months with an ERA under three, while Kimbrel had only three. Kimbrel also can be a bit more explosive, walking almost five batters per nine innings in 2018, while Jansen hovered right around two. Both of these guys are top of class, no doubt. Jansen's 2018 is creating a 2019 value, one that he hasn't had in a few years. I don't like paying for early saves, but if I do, I will bank on the guy who has the upside of being the league's top closer, and who comes at a cheaper cost. Jansen, first round KO.

CRAIG KIMBREL
BOGMAN

Well, we know that when buying a premium closer everything is going to be razor thin and with these guys it's business as usual. Jansen is coming off a down year because of his heart condition. Jansen's K/9 hit a career low of 10.3 (career 13.5), his ERA was also a career high of 3.01 and he just really didn't look right. Kimbrel is still a free agent right now but he is going to produce regardless of where he ends up. Kimbrel has at least 31 saves in every season since 2011, he has a K/9 over 13 in each of those seasons and has never gone over a 1.09 WHIP. They are both being drafted in the 65-75 range in NFBC drafts right now with Kimbrel being the higher of them. I really like both of these closers, Jansen being on one of the best teams in the NL makes it tough to pick against him for sure but, that heart condition is too scary for me to mess with. Give me the homeless Kimbrel in a close one 10-9.

★ ★ ★ WINNER - KENLEY JANSEN 10-9 ★ ★ ★

20 19

IN THIS LEAGUE
FANTASY SPORTS
PODCAST NETWORK

Judges Scorecard

JOE PISAPIA	ROB SILVER	CHRIS MEANEY
JANSEN 10-8	JANSEN 10-9	JANSEN 10-9

Round 26: Kenley Jansen vs Craig Kimbrel

WALKER BEUHLER VS CARLOS CARRASCO

WALKER BEUHLER			ROUND 27		CARLOS CARRASCO	
WINS	8				WINS	17
ERA	2.62 ★				ERA	3.38
WHIP	0.961 ★				WHIP	1.125
K	151				K	231
IP	137.1				IP	192.0

WALKER BEUHLER

THE WELSH

These two are going right next to each other in drafts. It's really interesting how the shine has come off of Carrasco a bit, and the way Buehler is being talked about by the smart people this year sounds very similar to the Carrasco love of days past. This isn't saying Buehler can't live up to the hype. When prospect eligible, Buehler topped out as my number one pitching prospect. Buehler did it hard in 2018. He had a monster second half dropping a 2.03 ERA, and raising his first to second half strikeout rate 4% to 29.9%. That would have ranked 8th in all of baseball, one spot a head of Carlos Carrasco. Buehler has been consistent with his arsenal, mixing all his pitches in the double digit range, and inducing ground balls with each pitch unlike most. The most effective jump was his slider, which he threw around 13% of the time. This resulted in his most effective swing strike pitch at over 15%. So let's take a break from the list of positive fundamental things we like about Buehler. Let's talk about the very surface level stuff. Buehler should have an innings cap, has a small track record and a lofty price. Carrasco has a proven track recorded, solid but not stellar 2018, and a team that is breaking up some of the band. Both going inside the top 40 overall for 2019. My friend CTM Baseball aka Matt Modica said something I really like about an article that a fellow friend, Ryan Bloomfield, wrote on Walker Buehler, "Don't draft scared, draft skills. Group think is not your friend. Buehler or bust!" It was related to Buehler vs Carrasco, and I am going to follow the upward trend. Buehler in a 10-9 decision.

CARLOS CARRASCO

BOGMAN

Walker Buehler is being called the next big thing and I'm buying into it for sure. He had an incredible rookie season and only got better in the 2nd half. Buehler is also setup with a great lineup and defense behind him as well and the Dodgers basically print money so he should have that for the majority of his career in LA. For as great as Walker Buehler is and should be this year Carrasco was better last year and I have no reason to believe that he won't be better this year as well. Buehler did have a better ERA than Carrasco last season but xFIP says that luck played a lot into that as Buehler was at 3.20 to Carrascos 2.90. BABIP also was hugely in Buehler's favor as we had the 6th lowest for pitchers with 120 or more IP at .248 while Carrasco was 16th highest at .315. If both of those BABIPs come back to the normal range of .275-.300ish Carrasco will be favored. Carrasco had the lower BB/9, higher K/9, higher SwStr% and plays in a division that features a lot of rebuilding teams in the White Sox, Royals, Tigers and Twins. These guys are both great and I have no problem in drafting Walker Buehler but for this year he's the guy you take if someone took Carrasco a few picks ahead of you. Carrasco takes it to the cards!

★ ★ ★ ★ WINNER - CARLOS CARRASCO 10-9 ★ ★ ★ ★

20 19 | Judges Scorecard

ALEX CHAMBERLAIN	JAMES ANDERSON	TIM HEANEY
CARRASCO 10-8	CARRASCO 10-9	BEUHLER 10-9

Round 27: Walker Beuhler vs Carlos Carrasco

MATT CARPENTER VS MIGUEL ANDÚJAR

	MATT CARPENTER		ROUND 28		MIGUEL ANDÚJAR	
AVG.	.257			★	AVG.	.297
HR	36	★			HR	27
RBI	81			★	RBI	92
RUNS	111	★			RUNS	83
SB	4	★			SB	2

MATT CARPENTER

THE WELSH

This is a tough one, because I am team Andújar, but am in Carpenter's corner for this matchup. Carpenter is proving to be a constant source of elite runs and and solid power. With his stolen bases being a non-factor, his RBI's and AVG go under the microscope. Roster Resource shows him leading off for the cards. Be it leadoff or two in front of Paul Goldschmidt, the runs should continue. He hit the ball harder and into the air more than he has at any point in his career, which lead to the career high 36 home runs. It could be his new recipe, but let's assume he comes down to earth, and we probably have sub 30 home runs. The leadoff spot is going to take significant RBI opportunities away and his average has never been elite. The addition of Paul Goldschmidt I believe will help both of these question marks. On the Andújar side, he did a lot right in 2018. He did everything but steal bases. He doesn't walk a lot, but if he continues making solid contact, it will impact him less than you'd expect. The power numbers might be inflated. Not counting August, he averaged about three home runs a month. In August he hit 10, which was as many as May, June and July combined. Low 20's might be his happy place. 80-90 on the runs and RBI's make him a solid option to go with his .280-.290 average. I'd also throw in a little side note that he has been rumored in trades, and he gets the home bump for sure. He hit .312 and a had 4% boost in HR/FB at home. Moving teams has a high probability of some form of a decrease. ADP's are close, and relatively reasonable to me. I might need Carpenter to poke an eye, or maybe put a knee to the groin, and for the judges not to see, but the best case is a 10-9 decision after 12 for Carpenter.

MIGUEL ANDÚJAR

BOGMAN

There are a lot of doubters for both of these guys for the 2019 season. It's basically an amazing somewhat unexpected year for Andújar vs a career/fully healthy year for Matt Carpenter. First off I'm not going to worry about the back stuff for Carpenter going into the season. Carp only missed 6 games last season so he clearly has conditioning or treatment down so that doesn't concern me at all. What does concern me about Carpenter is repeating his career high HR/FB rate of 19.1% and the career high K% of 23.3%. For the record I know that Carpenter has changed his swing and that led to these numbers, I'm just looking for repeatability of them. We keep hearing the Sophomore Slump term being thrown around with Andújar but I don't understand why. Andújar improved in the 2nd half of the season by 40 points in batting average AND hit more HRs in fewer games. With SBs probably being a wash as Carpenter's career high is 5 and Andújar not being a speedster, I think at best these guys split categories with Andújar definitely getting average and RBI as he hits lower in the middle of that Yankees lineup and Carpenter gets runs being that he is a leadoff hitter with HRs being in question. Either way I don't think that difference in HRs will make up for the 30ish points in average Andújar should walk away with (beat him by 40 last season). VERY tight one in Andújar's favor for upside.

★ ★ ★ WINNER - MATT CARPENTER 10-9 ★ ★ ★

Judges Scorecard

20 19

DEREK VAN RIPER	STEVE GARDNER	RYAN BLOOMFIELD
CARPENTER 10-9	CARPENTER 10-7	DRAW

Round 28: Matt Carpenter vs Miguel Andújar

ZACK GREINKE VS STEPHAN STRASBURG

	ZACK GREINKE		ROUND 29		STEPHAN STRASBURG
WINS	15 ★			WINS	10
ERA	3.21 ★			ERA	3.74
WHIP	1.079 ★			WHIP	1.200
K	199 ★			K	156
IP	207.2 ★			IP	130.0

ZACK GREINKE

THE WELSH

This is quite enjoyable, having to see Bogman argue Strasburg. To his credit, he's said it for like four straight years, and he's been right every time, Strasburg is good, but will get hurt. Four straight years now, Stras hasn't sniffed 200 innings pitched. He's only done it once in his career, in 2014. If we lived in a world where he could actually pitch 200 innings, Strasburg would be a top 10 fantasy pitcher. Low walks, high strikeouts and a solid team for run and win support. I want to believe. I give the benefit of doubt to a fault with injuries, but it just cannot be done with Strasburg. Greinke is the polar opposite. Four of the last five years, he's had 200 or more innings pitched. His stuff isn't at the same level of Strasburg, but his feel for pitching might be beyond strasburg "stuff." It takes all the innings to get Greinke to top 200 strikeouts, but he'll get there. Greinke's fastball velocity hit a low since 2004, which isn't great, but Greinke is going to bulldog his way at you. If he stays in Arizona, there should be worry about run support and wins (QS leagues can breathe easier). One last thing I'd say, is with the current ADP's in the 50-60 range, this actually is a great time to take a chance on Strasburg if there ever has been. The damage is so much less, but Greinke comes in at a lower cost and is about as dependable as they get. You can dream big here, but you may be going home. Greinke 5th round KO.

STEPHAN STRASBURG

BOGMAN

I've been campaigning against Strasburg since The Welsh and I fired up so no one is going to believe me anyway. While I may not be the biggest fan of Strasburg (or even a fan of Strasburg) he does throw quality innings. Strasburg has a better SwStr%, K/9, xFIP and likeability than Greinke. Strasburg is also in a more stable organization right now in Washington, really meaning we don't know if Greinke will stay in Arizona or be moved to a more or less favorable situation. Greinke had a solid season last year although, the humidor had close to no change for him at all. Greinke's ERA and WHIP were both up .01 from 2017, his K rate slipped a little bit while his BB rate fell and he still won 15 games which he has done in 8 of his last 15 seasons. Look, if I knew Strasburg was going to throw 200 innings he would be the easy victor in this one as he has the K upside and his ERA and WHIP are comparable to Greinke's. But, 'If if's and but's was candies and nuts we'd all have a Merry Christmas.' Take Strasburg if you feel lucky and if it works out send me lottery numbers.

★ ★ ★ WINNER - ZACK GREINKE 10-9 ★ ★ ★

2019

IN THIS LEAGUE · FANTASY SPORTS · PODCAST NETWORK

Judges Scorecard

CLAY LINK	KC BUBBA	JAKE CIELY
GREINKE 10-7	STRASBURG 10-9	DRAW

Round 29: Zack Greinke vs Stephan Strasburg

TOMMY PHAM VS A.J. POLLOCK

	TOMMY PHAM			ROUND		A.J. POLLOCK	
AVG.	.275 ★			**30**		AVG.	.257
HR	21					HR	21
RBI	63				★	RBI	65
RUNS	102 ★					RUNS	61
SB	15 ★					SB	13

TOMMY PHAM

THE WELSH

Pham has been underrated for years. He was moved to Tampa Bay late last year and absolutely destroyed the second half with a .331 average. His ADP has risen into the top 60. His power/speed combo, hot 2018 second half and middle of the order slot have fantasy owners excited. Not to try to defend AJ Pollock, but he shares a similar skill set. The injury-prone tag has been given to Pollock more than Pham. The ADP difference on these two muddies the waters a bit. Where Pham is top 60, Pollock was going around 120 in NFBC ADP. Steamer does not help, where these two are within three homers, four runs, 10 RBI, two stolen bases and .04 of average. Pollock is favored in all five of those categories. (Not that I am trying to make Scott's case for him.) I do think these two are closer than what ADP shows. Momentum has swung to Pham. Remember the second half numbers Pham had with his new team? Pollock is coming off a .233 second half, which was 50 points lower than the first half. Pollock also leaves hitter-friendly Arizona where he hit 40 points higher at home than on the road. When things are equal (I would say within 30 ADP spots) I am going to take momentum and Tommy Pham. 10-9 decision by the judges.

A.J. POLLOCK

BOGMAN

I need to work on my drafting habits when we are picking players here. The nice thing about this debate is that if the draft spots hold I actually DO believe in taking Pollock over Pham. As I'm typing this these guys are separated by 61 spots in NFBC drafts with Pham going at 59 and Pollock going at 120. I understand why everyone is so hyped on Pham, he had a really nice finish with the Rays last season, hitting .343 with 7 HRs and 5 SBs in only 39 games. Pollock was the opposite, really fading down the stretch and only hitting .233 in the second half. Landing in LA is going to be great for A.J. leading off for the Dodgers, hitting ahead of Seager, Turner and Bellinger is a coveted spot. Let's not forget the upside of Pollock even playing 24 fewer games than Pham he still tied him in HRs, RBI and was only 2 SBs behind Pham. Pham also hasn't been a paragon of health himself. Inside injuries has him down for 7 injuries last season. None of those injuries were season altering but it was enough to miss 25 games last year and he had the same story in 2017 with 6 injuries costing him 34 games. If these guys are within a round or two rounds of each other I would take Pham but 60 spots is too much as far as value goes. Give me Pollock at the current cost.

★ ★ ★ WINNER - TOMMY PHAM 10-7 ★ ★ ★

2019

IN THIS LEAGUE · FANTASY SPORTS · PODCAST NETWORK

Judges Scorecard

PAUL SPORER	JASON COLLETTE	ITL ARMY
PHAM 10-8	PHAM KO	PHAM 10-7 (77%)

Round 30: Tommy Pham vs A.J. Pollock

JEAN SEGURA VS XANDER BOGAERTS

	JEAN SEGURA		ROUND		XANDER BOGAERTS	
AVG.	.304	★			AVG.	.288
HR	10		**31**	★	HR	23
RBI	63			★	RBI	103
RUNS	91	★			RUNS	72
SB	20	★			SB	8

JEAN SEGURA

BOGMAN

I hate picking between these two because they are two of my favorite players in baseball. What I really love is my man Jean Segura moving back to the National League. The last time Segura was in the NL he hit 20 HRs and stole 30 bases. While that is not quite the return I expect for Segura this season it is in the realm of possible outcomes as Citizens Bank is 2nd over the last 3 years in HRs according to ballpark factors and teams tend to run more in the NL. The Phillies actually ran less than Seattle last season but they weren't exactly flush with base stealers as Cesar Hernandez led with 19 and Quinn and Kingery tied for 2nd at 10. They have added Cutch to go with Segura at the top of the lineup and are working on adding more so I would have to assume the SB will be in heavier rotation. It looks like we can figure this one out pretty simply, Segura will win SB and Runs, Bogaerts will run HRs and RBI and batting average will be the deciding factor. Over the last 3 seasons Segura has won batting average every single season, he has the upside to be close in HRs to Xander, will steal more bases AND he's going 2 rounds later than Bogaerts. I love Xander but this an easy KO victory for Segura.

XANDER BOGAERTS

THE WELSH

Xander Bogaerts seems like he changes his narrative on a yearly basis. 2016 seemed to be the start of the real Bogaerts, and over the last three years he teased us with the areas he might excel in. He has gone from 10 HR to 23 HR, 72 runs to 115 runs, 62 RBI to 103 RBI and 8 SB to 23 SB. All these stats have swung around over the last three years. Bogaerts was a bit more aggressive with his swing in 2018. He hit the ball harder and showed a 6.5% rise in hard hit percentage. The HR/FB rate rise drove an increase in home runs. Since 2017 was kind of the down year, I look at what was different in 2017 from 2016 and 2018. One thing that stood out was his first pitch strike percentage. It was down almost five percentage points from the year before, while 2017 was down about 3% from 2016. This might have to do with the order of the lineup as well. In 2016 Bogaerts mainly hit out of the three hole, with some at bats in the two hole as well. In 2017 he hit between leadoff and sixth. Last year he played 110 games batting fourth or fifth. Bogaerts has to adjust in the lineup more often than most. I think he is settling into a .285-20-75-90-10 floor player. Segura in a new spot opens up possibilities, but he is on a three year decrease in home runs and stolen bases. Philly opens up new hopes, but I do not see the upside with Segura. Bogaerts will win three of five categories easily, and the ones Segura win will not be of enough value to swing to his side. First round KO Bogaerts over Segura.

★ ★ ★ WINNER - JEAN SEGURA 10-9 ★ ★ ★

20 19

Judges Scorecard

IN THIS LEAGUE · FANTASY SPORTS · PODCAST NETWORK

JOE PISAPIA	ROB SILVER	SAMMY REID
SEGURA 10-9	**BOGAERTS 10-9**	**SEGURA 10-9**

Round 31: Jean Segura vs Xander Bogaerts

JAMES PAXTON VS PATRICK CORBIN

	JAMES PAXTON		ROUND 32			PATRICK CORBIN
WINS	11				WINS	11
ERA	3.76			★	ERA	3.15
WHIP	1.098			★	WHIP	1.050
K	208			★	K	246
IP	160.1			★	IP	200.0

JAMES PAXTON
THE WELSH

For a few years now I have been in the "James Paxton is better than anyone will admit" camp. He has put together two consecutive seasons of high quality fantasy production. The biggest knock is the time he missed. Paxton has averaged just under 150 innings over the last two years. Steamer will only give the new Yankee a projection of 172 innings in 2019. If Paxton gets to 200 innings, he will strike out 250+. With that Yankee offense, Paxton will probably also be sporting a 16 to 17 win season. That would put him in the conversation for a top 10 2019 pitcher. Ifs and buts, right? The thing that hurts this fight, is Corbin did most of everything I just said last year. He went from essentially a two-pitch average pitcher, to two plus pitches (slider was A+) and added a curveball that made him dominate. The move up was so dramatic, it is going to leave some questioning the reality of it this year. I will be honest, though, Corbin's breakout looks more real than anything. Paxton just has two years under his belt, and now a more powerful offense for support. They are going in the same round, but Paxton has the narrow edge for me with a 10-9 decision.

PATRICK CORBIN
BOGMAN

My Patrick Corbin love finally paid off! That and the fact that he scrapped the change for a curveball and threw his best pitch (slider) way more in 2018. Corbin had career bests in everything but wins in 2018 after the change which should improve for him being on a much better Nationals team this year. Paxton did the same thing though, he scraped his change and threw his cutter way more and saw improvements in Ks/9 and SwStr% and he parlayed that into being traded to the Yankees. Corbin is also on the move but seeing that Yankee Stadium and Nationals Park have the 1st and 5th worst park factors for pitchers this doesn't really give anyone a solid lead. If I knew these guys would both start a season full of games I would give Corbin the slightest of edges over Paxton, better xFIP, better SwStr% and lower BB% should translate to any ballpark. It's really the fact that Paxton hasn't started 30 games ever and the most innings he's pitched was last season at 160.1. Corbin has started 30+ the last two seasons and has looked stronger every year since undergoing TJ surgery in 2014. These pitchers are very similar in value this season and are going within 4 spots of each other in NFBC drafts but I give the slight edge to Corbin due to Paxton's missed starts every season of his career.

★ ★ ★ WINNER - PATRICK CORBIN 10-9 ★ ★ ★

2019

Judges Scorecard

ENO SARRIS	STEVE GARDNER	TIM HEANEY
CORBIN 10-9	CORBIN 10-9	CORBIN 10-9

Round 32: James Paxton vs Patrick Corbin

LORENZO CAIN VS VÍCTOR ROBLES

	LORENZO CAIN		ROUND	VÍCTOR ROBLES	
AVG.	.308	★		AVG.	.276
HR	10	★	**33**	HR	2
RBI	38	★		RBI	14
RUNS	90	★		RUNS	32
SB	30	★		SB	19

2018 MiLB Stats

LORENZO CAIN
BOGMAN

The good ole shiny new toy versus the grizzled veteran! Robles is going about 30 spots below Cain but we all know pre season hype will move Robles up the chain and this will be much closer than that at draft time. Robles has tons of upside for sure but for me he is too much of an unknown for me to suggest taking him inside the top 100 players. Robles is of course a highly touted prospect but the Nationals are stacked at OF options and even if Robles gets the majority of the starts he is most likely going to be hitting at the bottom of the Nats lineup. The worry with Cain is age and missing games. Cain will be 33 shortly after the beginning of the season and has only played 150 games in a season once in his career but he did play in 140 games last year and has hit that mark 3 of the last 4 seasons. Cain hits leadoff one spot ahead of the reigning MVP in one of the best offenses in the NL and he stole a career high 30 bases last season and hit double digit HRs for only the 3rd time in his career. The questionable playing time, low spot in the batting order and overall unknown of Robles make this an easy Cain victory. I'm not against taking both of these guys but if I have to pick one it's Cain taking it 10-7.

VÍCTOR ROBLES
THE WELSH

For all the love prospects have gotten over the last two years, from Ronald Acuna last year to Vlad, Jr. and Eloy this year, there has been very little fanfare for Víctor Robles. This should not be the case. Robles is an outfielder with plus tools who should excel in batting average and stolen bases. Similar to Cain, the power is the question we need answered. I can tell you the power can get there for Robles. When I saw him during the Arizona Fall League, his approach and bat speed rivaled that of even Ronald Acuna. Can Robles tap into it? We will have to see. At this stage in his career, he actually looks very much like a young Lorenzo Cain. The difference to dream on might be the upside. Cain has been as consistent as they come. Though not quite elite in any area, Cain returns three above average categories in average, stolen bases and runs. His home runs totals are more than reasonable, but his RBI totals have continued a three run downturn which left with him only 38 all last year. Steamer is pretty generous to Cain this coming year predicting a return of most of his 2018 output with almost double the RBI. In fact, Steamer shows Cain and Robles with very similar production. Cain is better in home runs, while stolen bases favor Robles. The projections all seem reasonable, though I could see Robles sacrifice some average for more power. If not, Robles may hover around a .300 average in 2019. What turns the debate is cost. Cain is going around 30 spots more expensive than Robles. You are paying for consistent output with Cain. I want that similar production with more upside on all categories except average. I am a firm believer in Robles for 2019, and in his corner for the 10-8 win over Cain.

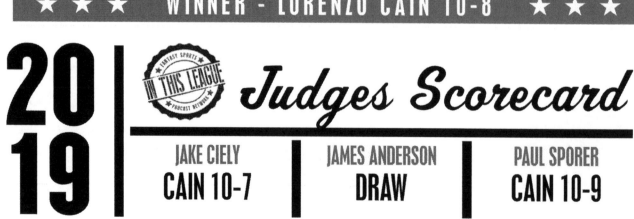

★ ★ ★ **WINNER - LORENZO CAIN 10-8** ★ ★ ★

20 19 | **Judges Scorecard**

IN THIS LEAGUE
FANTASY SPORTS PODCAST NETWORK

JAKE CIELY	JAMES ANDERSON	PAUL SPORER
CAIN 10-7	DRAW	CAIN 10-9

WIL MYERS VS YASIEL PUIG

	WIL MYERS		ROUND 34		YASIEL PUIG
AVG.	.253			★ AVG.	.267
HR	11			★ HR	23
RBI	39			★ RBI	63
RUNS	39			★ RUNS	60
SB	13			★ SB	15

WIL MYERS

BOGMAN

It's the unlikeable Bowl! Unfortunately both of these guys are probably going to be decent adds to your fantasy team this year. These two have the same power/speed skill set with average not being their strongest of traits as neither of them have hit .270 in the past 4 seasons. Wil Myers is coming off an oblique strain and foot injury that cost him almost half of the season but the good news is he played pretty much all of September so he'll be all set at the start of spring training. I like the fact that Puig was traded away from LA but going to Cincinnati isn't the best situation because they will probably rotate between their 4 OFs in Puig, Kemp, Schebler and Winker. The good news for Puig is that he really surged at the end of last season and he will at least have the chance to earn a permanent starting gig. Myers will slide back into the cleanup spot in San Diego AND he will qualify at 3B this season after getting in 36 games there last season. I have seen these guys go within 9 spots of each other on one platform and as much as 46 spots on another. Myers is just way more stable than Puig, he's a cleanup hitter with multiple position eligibility who's last healthy season saw him go 30/20 while Puig is an 8 hole hitter in an OF rotation in a new situation. Puig has to land the desperation punch to win this one which is possible but not likely.

YASIEL PUIG

THE WELSH

I am a big #PuigYourFriend guy. Puig has had some maturity issues amongst other things, but I have always been team Puig. That makes this debate funny, as I have equally been NOT on team Myers. Bogman and I have razzed Wil Myers for years out here in Arizona due to his salty attitude with fans and overall demeanor. This is not to say Myers has not been a valuable asset. 20/20 seasons from qualified 1B have not come often. This year those 1B qualifications will be gone, though Myers did add 3B. The Padres came out and said Myers will play full-time in the outfield, while filling in at other spots when needed. Puig is off to his new home with the Reds. I am not sure there was one player who needed a change of scenery more than him. The lack of commitment from the Dodgers has always hurt his value. Regardless, Team Puig finished with his second straight 20 HR, 15 SB season. Moving to Cincinnati, in my eyes, is a big win. Puig last season hit 50 points lower at home, and now moves to hitter-friendly Cincinnati. This is speculation, but the idea of him working with one of the hardest-working hitters in baseball in Joey Votto seems like a huge plus. I imagine Votto will hit in front of him, opening up a world of new RBI opportunities on a regular basis. I think there is a career year in all five categories coming for Puig. Myers's slowdown last year leads me to believe a few more bumps in the road are coming. Puig with a 10-8 decision. #PuigYourPick

★ ★ ★ WINNER - YASIEL PUIG 10-9 ★ ★ ★

20 19 | IN THIS LEAGUE | Judges Scorecard

CLAY LINK	NATE GRIMM	CHRIS MEANEY
PUIG 10-9	PUIG 10-9	PUIG 10-8

Round 34: Wil Myers vs Yasiel Puig

MARCELL OZUNA VS JUSTIN UPTON

	MARCELL OZUNA			JUSTIN UPTON	
AVG.	.280	★	AVG.	.257	
HR	23		★ HR	30	
RBI	88	★	RBI	85	
RUNS	69		★ RUNS	80	
SB	3		★ SB	8	

ROUND 35

MARCELL OZUNA

THE WELSH

I was surprised when I looked at how consistent Justin Upton has been over the last six years. It has not always been great (for example, Upton's average) but with some variations of RBI/Runs you can count on around a 30-85-85-10 season. This performance is well worth the draft cost if you can take the hit in batting average. Ozuna does not have the track record Upton has, but he has had a few great seasons. A big knock on Ozuna is how his astronomical 2017 dropped off in 2018. He dropped 30 points of average, 14 home runs, 30 runs and 40 RBI. If you counted on the 2017 line last year was a disappointment, even though 2018 was more in line with his 2016. I am hopeful on Ozuna. He hit the ball harder and made better contact last year, but had his lowest HR/FB rate since 2015. Ozuna finished 2018, though, hitting 30 points higher on his average and raised his HR/FB rate from a first half 10% to 17%. Balance new, realistic expectations with the second half positives and mix them in Ozuna's one big advantage in batting average, and you see Ozuna is a clear-cut winner. Goldschmidt's addition to the lineup should create more offense and possible protection as well. Upton may take a slight lead on home run, RBI and run totals, but the average is such a huge gap, it helps the judges give Ozuna a 10-7 win!

JUSTIN UPTON

BOGMAN

Justin Upton is very predictable, he's going to score and drive in 80-100 runs, hit 30ish HRs and steal 10ish bases all while hitting somewhere around .265. Upton is and always will be a very streaky player, last season in back to back months he hit .301 and then .197. Ozuna is the question, after an amazing 2017 season in Miami where he hit .312 with 37 HRs and 124 RBI he was traded to a better lineup and friendlier hitters park in St. Louis and he dropped 14 HRs, 36 RBI and 31 points in batting average. Ozuna did have a shoulder surgery in late October so we can't be sure how much that plagued him last season but he was said to be dealing with it for most of the year. Of course if it was really bad why would he wait until a month after the season to fix it plus he actually hit better in the 2nd half with more power. The underlying numbers can't even settle this one, Upton strikes out more, Upton also walks more, Upton has a higher career HR/FB ratio and ISO, Ozuna makes more hard contact but also more soft contact and their career SwStr% is within .01 of each other. I think bottom line between these guys is Ozuna has the higher ceiling and Upton has the higher floor. Give me the consistent dude not coming off shoulder surgery, Upton in a close one.

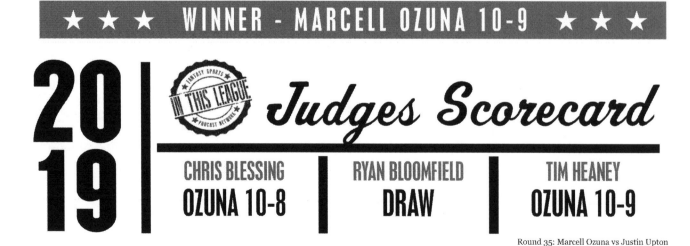

★ ★ ★ WINNER - MARCELL OZUNA 10-9 ★ ★ ★

2019

Judges Scorecard

CHRIS BLESSING	RYAN BLOOMFIELD	TIM HEANEY
OZUNA 10-8	DRAW	OZUNA 10-9

Round 35: Marcell Ozuna vs Justin Upton

JOSÉ ABREU VS EDWIN ENCARNACIÓN

	JOSÉ ABREU			ROUND		EDWIN ENCARNACIÓN	

AVG.	.265 ★			AVG.	.246
HR	22		★	HR	32
RBI	78		★	RBI	107
RUNS	68		★	RUNS	74
SB	2		★	SB	3

ROUND 36

JOSÉ ABREU

THE WELSH

We might be closing in on the ol' dusty trail for nickname favorite E5. We are not in a spot where we would call Encarnación finished, but we are on a three year decline that has seen his home runs fall from 42 to 32, runs from 99 to 72 and average fall from .263 to .246. As of writing this, Encarnación's home is with the Mariners, which is less than ideal for his value. Even if he gets a new home by opening day, we need to temper expectations for the 36 year-old. José Abreu is coming off of a down year. This was mostly due to injury, but he ran into some bad luck with a 30 point drop in his BABIP from the previous three years. The small dip in contact and hard hit rate could be the beginning of a bad trend. It could also have been some of the symptoms of bad luck and injury. Abreu (like E5, to be fair) finished the year on a high note, hitting .293 in the second half. Unlike E5, Abreu has been a constant source for home runs, RBI, runs and average. In 2017, when E5 hit .256, Abreu sported a .307 average. If all you cared about were the home runs, RBI and runs, ADP favors the value of E5 by quite a bit. The difference in the average is a game charger, and outweighs the multi round difference. José Abreu in 6th round KO over E5.

EDWIN ENCARNACIÓN

BOGMAN

I'd like to quote the great James Franco from the Interview for this debate 'Same, Same... but different!' Power hitting first baseman in less than ideal lineups with the potential to be traded. They both missed games last season with Abreu (hernia surgery) finishing at 128 games and Encarnacion (multiple small injuries) at 137. Despite missing his most games since 2014 Encarnacion was able to hit 30+ HRs and drive in 98+ for the 7th straight season in a row. 2018 was the first season Abreu didn't get to at least 25 HRs or 100 RBI because of the injury. Abreu also had the lowest batting average he has had in the bigs at .265 but Encarnacion had his lowest since 2010 and it's dropped the past 4 straight seasons. The underlying numbers are close as well, Abreu has a higher Contact%, Encarnacion makes more Hard Contact, the SwStr% was almost identical, they even both had similar split stats. The two biggest differences is that Abreu is about 4 years younger but he's also going 2 rounds ahead of Encarnacion. I'm not against taking both of these guys but if I have to pick one give me Encarnacion. He has the higher career ISO between these guys and is likely to be moved to a better lineup.

★ ★ ★ WINNER - JOSÉ ABREU 10-8 ★ ★ ★

20 19

IN THIS LEAGUE
FANTASY SPORTS PODCAST NETWORK

Judges Scorecard

JOE PISAPIA	DEREK VAN RIPER	SAMMY REID
ABREU 10-8	ABREU 10-8	E5 10-9

Round 36: José Abreu vs Edwin Encarnación

CHRIS ARCHER VS CARLOS MARTÍNEZ

	CHRIS ARCHER		ROUND 37		CARLOS MARTÍNEZ	
WINS	6			★	WINS	8
ERA	4.31			★	ERA	3.11
WHIP	1.375			★	WHIP	1.348
K	162	★			K	117
IP	148.1	★			IP	118.2

CHRIS ARCHER

BOGMAN

This one is all over the place. Martínez is going ahead of Archer by 10 spots in some places and 30 in others depending on the provider. These two might be switching spots if we were looking at the underlying numbers, Martínez smoked Archer in ERA 3.11 to 4.31 but xFIP went the other way with Archer winning 3.59 to 4.42. Archer also took SwStr%, K/9. and BB/9 and the underlying stats he was beat in wasn't by much. The other knock against Carlos Martínez is that after he returned from his oblique strain the Cards moved him to the bullpen. The plan coming into spring training is for Carlos Martínez to be a starter this season but should the bullpen become a problem or if he has another injury the bullpen has now become an option for him. I have to give up that St. Louis is the better spot to pick up a cheap win over Pittsburgh and like I've said before we don't count the underlying numbers so winning xFIP doesn't matter if it doesn't match up to actual ERA but these are the more 'trustable' numbers for the upcoming season. Honestly, both of these guys will be over drafted this season but if I have to bank on one it will be Archer but the scorecard would be like 8-7.

CARLOS MARTÍNEZ

THE WELSH

Carlos Martínez was on his way to establishing himself as one of the premier young arms in baseball in 2018. He was coming off a three and a half ERA, 200 inning, 200 strikeout season, with a career high K/9 and a career low in BB/9. When 2018 rolled around, it seemed he was hit with injuries every month. Martínez went to the DL in May with a lat strain, the DL in July with an oblique issue, and when he came off the DL in August, he managed to get the wind knocked out of him by a 109 MPH liner to his chest. His return in August saw him move into the bullpen for the final month or so of the season. It was a disaster of a year. Martínez is moving back to the rotation in 2019 with an ADP well outside of the top 100. It is hard to know how seriously to weigh the negatives in Martínez's 2018 stats due to his injuries. If you believe he is no longer a viable starting pitcher option, you could cite his drop in velocity and the loss of command which resulted in a career-worst 4.55 BB/9. I am a firm believer in Car-Mart. Though he struggled in 2018, the ground balls he induces are a calling card to get of jams when he gets a bit wild. He is a sneaky source of strikeouts and can go deep into games. I share some similar feelings on Archer, maybe more that it is popular to hate him than to covet him, especially at his high price. Carlos Martínez does not suffer the same same fastball issues we see from Archer. Injuries, friends, injuries. If Martínez can put the injury bug in his back pocket, I think we see a career year in wins, ERA and strikeouts. Martínez is a big target of mine, and a 10-7 winner over Archer.

★ ★ ★ ★ WINNER - CARLOS MARTÍNEZ 10-8 ★ ★ ★ ★

20 19

Judges Scorecard

ALEX CHAMBERLAIN	NICK POLLACK	JAMES ANDERSON
ARCHER 10-9	MARTÍNEZ KO	MARTÍNEZ 10-9

Round 37: Chris Archer vs Carlos Martínez

EUGENIO SUAREZ VS ANTHONY RENDON

	EUGENIO SUAREZ		ROUND		ANTHONY RENDON	
AVG.	.283			★ AVG.	.308	
HR	34 ★		**38**	HR	24	
RBI	104 ★			RBI	92	
RUNS	79			★ RUNS	88	
SB	1			★ SB	2	

EUGENIO SUÁREZ

BOGMAN

I finally have to give up on my Anthony Rendon hate. My initial problem with Rendon coming in to the draft from Rice was that he had chronic ankle problems. The ankle issues kept him to under 100 games in two of his first 3 seasons at the big league level but the past 3 seasons he has played at least 136 games. The 26 games he missed last season were because of wrist and foot issues but Suárez missed 19 games due to different nagging issues but most of those were early in the season. Rendon makes crazy high contact, his z-contact% (contact on pitches swung at in the strike zone) was in the top 20 among qualified batters last season. Suárez was no slouch though as his z-contact% was in the top 60 and he made a significant amount of hard contact at 48.6% which was tied for 2nd among qualified hitters in the league last year. Most of the other numbers are so close that this really comes down to power vs average. Suárez has improved his HR and RBI numbers every year of his career but he is not the average hitter that Rendon is. As with all debates I will lean towards the power over basically everything and Suárez seems to have more of it. They are being drafted relatively close together in all formats I have seen so a razor thing victory in the cards goes to Suárez.

ANTHONY RENDON

THE WELSH

Make me choose one of my children why don't you, geez! Annually underrated third basemen, both Anthony Rendon and Eugenio Suárez are going to get their shot in 2019, at a premium price. Suárez has continued to rise in home run output, RBI and batting average over the last three years. Rendon himself has seen his average rise to a career-high .308. More than anything else he has leveled and maintained consistent output across five categories that you can count on (not that either gives you stolen bases.) Regardless of his .280 average in 2018, I do not buy Suárez as a consistent option for that category. A Steamer-projected dip into the mid .250s makes more sense. Suárez had 6% jump in HR/FB percentage and hit the ever-living crap out of the ball improving his hard hit rate from 33% to 48%. Even when he levels off a bit, the ball is still going to fly. The ball does the same for Rendon, just not at the same clip. What brings me back to Rendon is the way he approaches his at-bats, with contact! Rendon was top 20 in contact % inside the zone, and sports a 5% swinging strike rate. The philosophy is: solid at-bats, get one base, don't make mistakes and produce consistently. I agree Suárez is underrated, and I like the 30 home run potential at the hot corner. I am not sure the difference in those counting stats outweighs the massive jump in average that comes with Rendon, especially considering the ADPs are within a round of each other. Look for a career year from Rendon, and do not look back on the average. Rendon with a 10-7 decision.

★ ★ ★ **WINNER - ANTHONY RENDON 10-9** ★ ★ ★

20 19

Judges Scorecard

PAUL SPORER	STEVE GARDNER	CLAY LINK
RENDON 10-9	**RENDON 10-8**	**RENDON 10-9**

Round 38: Eugenio Suárez vs Anthony Rendon

GARY SÁNCHEZ VS J.T. REALMUTO

	GARY SÁNCHEZ			ROUND 39			J.T. REALMUTO	
AVG.	.186					★ AVG.	.277
HR	18					★ HR	21
RBI	53					★ RBI	74
RUNS	51					★ RUNS	74
SB	1					★ SB	3

GARY SÁNCHEZ

THE WELSH

No player with 350 or more plate appearances in all of baseball had a lower BABIP than Gary Sánchez. In fact he was the only player to sport a BABIP under .200. Poor contact when he was not hitting it out of the park, missed time and bad luck were the 2018 story for Sánchez. We can hope for regression to the superb 2017 season that vaulted his value into the late second to early third round. That ridiculously low BABIP alone is a huge indicator of a bounce back in 2018. Steamer agrees, projecting him to improve to a .245 average and 30 home runs. J.T. Realmuto represents consistency with a .275 average or better in three of the last four years, with comparable run and home run numbers. The power clearly works in Sánchez's favor, and the RBI should be a separator if you believe Sánchez returns mostly to form. My main issue with both of these guys is they still cost a premium. NFBC ADP has them both inside the 50-60 range. From a draft strategy standpoint, there is no way I invest in a catcher inside the top 80 or maybe even top 100. The catcher position has dwindled in value, which will make some press to have one of the few "elite" catchers, but I believe both these two are far from elite fantasy players. Realmuto's consistency is intriguing, especially at what has become a volatile position, but Sánchez's upside is undeniable. He is a year removed from hitting 33 home runs, 90 RBI with a .278 average in just 122 games. There is little to no doubt in my mind Sánchez outperforms last year. This alone gives Sánchez the edge over Realmuto. I don't think we see 2017 Sánchez, but I do think we see a 3 to 5 category lead for Sánchez, and a more than serviceable average. Sánchez with a 10-8 win.

J.T. REALMUTO

BOGMAN

I don't think I'll own either one of these guys in redrafts this year. Taking a catcher high is just not a priority of mine. I play in almost no 2 catcher leagues so I'll just usually wait until the final few rounds to make a catcher pick and then see who rises to the top of the wire and add that guy. With that being said I can't be talked into taking Realmuto where he's going but he is a great value compared to other catchers, he checks all the boxes although his SBs have gone down 3 straight seasons and he probably can't be counted on for them anymore. Gary Sánchez just had such a pathetic 2018 season I don't understand how he's climbing into the top 100 talk again and I was all in last season. I know he had shoulder surgery in the off season and some people are going to point to that as the thing that will have him back on track this season but the shoulder bothered him in 2017 when he was dropping those 30 bombs. Sánchez can be a big difference maker but I just can't bank on him getting the average back to .275 and hitting 25 HRs and that is what we are paying for when we buy him at that price. I don't want to take Realmuto at his cost but I can bank on him hitting in the mid .270s at least and probably 20 bombs AND he should end up in a much better lineup sooner rather than later. Realmuto on a technicality.

★ ★ ★ WINNER - GARY SÁNCHEZ 10-9 ★ ★ ★

20 19 | *Judges Scorecard*

IN THIS LEAGUE — FANTASY SPORTS PODCAST NETWORK

ROB SILVER	JAKE CIELY	EDDY ALMAGUER
SÁNCHEZ 10-9	REALMUTO 10-9	SÁNCHEZ 10-9

Round 39: Gary Sánchez vs J.T. Realmuto

JACK FLAHERTY VS ZACK WHEELER

JACK FLAHERTY

WINS	8		
ERA	3.34		
WHIP	1.106	★	
K	182	★	
IP	151.0		

ROUND 40

ZACK WHEELER

★	WINS	12
★	ERA	3.31
	WHIP	1.124
	K	179
★	IP	182.1

JACK FLAHERTY

THE WELSH

Jack Flaherty is a popular name this year. There always seem to be those "next step" starting pitchers ranked between 20 and 30. In fact both Flaherty and Zack Wheeler sit in that range. They took big steps in 2018, so we are going to have to pay a premium for 2019. Wheeler's second half featured a 1.68 ERA and an almost 3% higher K%. Flaherty did not flash in the second half, but was consistent throughout the season. Of pitchers who had 150 or more innings in 2018, Flaherty ranked 10th in K% with a 29.6%, better than guys like Luis Severino, Aaron Nola and Corey Kluber. He also had the 13th-best swinging strike percentage. Flaherty's main issues came from lack of control. He had a walk rate about 2% higher than Wheeler. Flaherty's fastball might not be on par with Wheeler's, but his slider proved to be top-notch. If we simply looked at the players, I would call this a KO for Flaherty. Though I have seen some smart rankers have these guys next to each other, Wheeler is coming in about 30 spots lower in ADP. That is a difficult deal to beat. The difference for me is my number one target in fantasy pitchers -- strikeouts. Flaherty's 10.84 K/9 is dramatically higher than Wheeler's 8.84 K/9. With an improvement in command, Flaherty moves this debate heavily in his favor. This is a blow for blow 12 round slobberknocker. 10-9 Flaherty by the judges.

ZACK WHEELER

BOGMAN

I LOVE this debate for Wheeler because it is probably the easiest one to argue so far in this book. These guys are pretty close to identical, they are .03 off in ERA, .01 in WHIP, Flaherty had a better K rate but Wheeler had mores Ws and the underlying stats are mostly split too. Flaherty had a better SwStr%, Wheeler induced more soft contact and had a better GB/FB ratio. The big split comes in the second half of the season in 2018. Flaherty didn't hit the wall his first full season in the bigs at all, he maintained his ERA (only rising by .2) and he improved his K rate in the second half. Zack Wheeler added a splitter to his repertoire this season and no one could handle it as he got used to mixing it in in the 2nd half. Wheeler's ERA dropped from 4.44 in the 1st half to 1.68 in the second half, he went at least 7 innings in his last 6 starts of which 5 were quality. I am a self admitted strikeout whore and will usually gravitate towards the sexy strikeout numbers but I want to see what Wheeler can do with a full offseason of working on that split AND he's being drafted at least 30 picks after Flaherty at current draft prices. This one is a first round drop for Wheeler, KO BITCH!!

★ ★ ★ WINNER - JACK FLAHERTY 10-9 ★ ★ ★

20 19 Judges Scorecard

JASON COLLETTE	SAMMY REID	NATE GRIMM
FLAHERTY 10-9	FLAHERTY 10-8	WHEELER 10-9

Round 40: Jack Flaherty vs Zack Wheeler

JOSH DONALDSON VS MATT CHAPMAN

	JOSH DONALDSON			MATT CHAPMAN
AVG.	.246		★ AVG.	.278
HR	8	ROUND **41**	★ HR	24
RBI	23		★ RBI	68
RUNS	30		★ RUNS	100
SB	2 ★		SB	1

JOSH DONALDSON
BOGMAN

Matt Chapman finally got in a full season of ABs and really came through for the A's and fantasy owners last season. Not only that but Chapman was also a steal last season in the draft so if you had him last season AND everything seems to be repeatable outside of the high BABIP (.338). I'm probably going to look like a snake oil salesman trying to talk you into buying Donaldson again this season but between these two I will be spending my pick on him. I'm not saying that he is 100% healthy but he played the last month of the season for the Indians and looked great. Donaldson is a former MVP with at least 30 HRs for the 3 seasons before 2018 and he's being drafted in the early 100s right now. This one probably comes down to where you have taken your risks up to this point in the draft. Safe drafts should take a risk with Donaldson and risky drafts should take Chapman for the high floor. Donaldson on the one year 'prove it' deal is what has me a little extra excited for him, he has more incentive to play through the nagging injuries and there is no DH to bail him out this year. To the cards we go again for this one but I'll take Donaldson in the slimmest of margins.

MATT CHAPMAN
THE WELSH

If you are looking for depth at a position, I would not call third base the Grand Canyon, but at least it is deeper than first base. If you are looking to save a few bucks, these two are probably in your sights. Matt Chapman is on the upswing. Chapman made solid adjustments from his partial-year rookie season to his sophomore full season. He lowered his strikeouts by 5%, raised his batting average 40 points and put the ball in the air more. Chapman had a solid second half of the season, hitting 50 points higher and raising his HR/FB rate almost 5%. Steamer sees some regression coming, but one clear advantage is his transformation into more of a home run hitter. Maybe I am in a camp of my own here, but he kind of reminds me of a young Josh Donaldson. This year is tough to predict with Donaldson. If you throw out his injury-plagued 2018, he has not shown many signs of slowing down. The injuries are definitely a problem. He has essentially played one season's worth of games over the last two years. If you believe he is not going quietly into the night, than the price has never been better. These two are both going after pick 100. Taking Chapman and Donaldson as your 3B and CI might be a win-win situation. The lack of trust in average is keeping Chapman's ADP down, but we do not usually get discounts on middle of the order power-hitting third basemen with their arrow ticking up (last year's Rafael Devers is an example). While I like them both, if I am choosing one, I easily take the upside on Chapman. Chapman is coming off a smoking-hot second half, much better than the injury-plagued 33 year old. Chapman with a 10-7 victory.

★ ★ ★ **WINNER - MATT CHAMPAN 10-9** ★ ★ ★

20 19

Judges Scorecard

JOE PISAPIA	ENO SARRIS	RYAN BLOOMFIELD
DONALDSON 10-8	CHAPMAN 10-8	CHAPMAN 10-9

Round 41: Josh Donaldson vs Matt Chapman

JAMESON TAILLON VS MADISON BUMGARNER

	JAMESON TAILLON		ROUND 42		MADISON BUMGARNER
WINS	14 ★			WINS	6
ERA	3.20 ★			ERA	3.26
WHIP	1.178 ★			WHIP	1.242
K	179 ★			K	109
IP	191.0 ★			IP	129.2

JAMESON TAILLON
THE WELSH

Jameson Taillon made a fantastic jump in 2018. The biggest change was the addition of a slider to his arsenal. Taillon threw the slider about 18% of the time and it became a critical piece to his success and his uptick in strikeouts. Taillon did not blow anyone away in strikeout totals. He still had around an 8.5 K/9, but did see his swinging strike percentage jump from 8.2 to 10.7% year over year. His overall strikeout percentage jumped from 21.3% to 22.8%. One of the more encouraging signs to me was the drop in his walk rate, down from 3.10 BB/9 to 2.10. That translates to his walk percentage dropping from 7.8% to 5.9% (tied for 13th lowest in baseball). Taillon made the moves you make when you jump from average to above-average major league pitcher. Madison Bumgarner had been above average for so many years until the last two. Injuries have been a major problem. MadBum's fastball velocity fell to the second lowest of his career. His swinging strike rate fell below 10% and was the second lowest of his career. If you compare Bumgarner to Kershaw -- who I have a lot of faith in this year -- even when Kershaw struggles he still finds success. Bumgarner has not found a way to do the same. Bumgarner's xFIP increased by a run, he had his lowest K/9 since 2010 and he had the highest BB/9 of his career at 2.98. I will not put it past Bumgarner to make adjustments, but for now Bumgarner and Taillon are going in the same range at around SP19/SP20. I can see myself having some shares of Bumgarner this season, but Taillon is checking all the right boxes for me. I think he continues to build on his strikeout numbers this year, leading to a 10-8 win for Taillon.

MADISON BUMGARNER
BOGMAN

We just want a healthy offseason from Bumgarner so we can know if this string of injuries plus the innings total in his career is really piling up on him and he's really cooked. He has only suffered two injuries in the last two years but they were really bad, the ATV accident that cost him about 15 starts in 17 and the broken hand right before the season started last year that cost him about 11 starts. Last season we saw him mix his pitches way differently than he has in the past as well, which led to more ground balls but fewer Ks. Taillon had his first full year of starts and he came through as well with a great season and I don't see why he can't come close to those numbers this season. Before the past two years Bumgarner hit 200+ innings in 6 straight seasons and struckout at least 191 in all of those seasons. I don't have anything negative to say about Taillon I just don't think he should be a top 65 player with only one full season of starts under his belt. Bumgarner is unbelievably risky and honestly might not be worth a top 75 pick either but we know the ceiling is great. A lot like the Donaldson debate this one is about the risk you are willing to take and this is my area to be a risk taker. Bumgarner in the cards!

★ ★ ★ WINNER - JAMESON TAILLON 10-8 ★ ★ ★

20
19

Judges Scorecard

KC BUBBA	DEREK VAN RIPER	CHRIS MEANEY
TAILLON 10-7	TAILLON 10-7	BUMGARNER 10-9

Round 42: Jameson Taillon vs Madison Bumgarner

BLAKE TREINEN VS EDWIN DIAZ

	BLAKE TREINEN		ROUND 43		EDWIN DIAZ	
SAVES	38			★	SAVES	57
ERA	0.78 ★				ERA	1.96
WHIP	0.834			★	WHIP	0.791
SO	100			★	SO	124
IP	80.1 ★				IP	73.1

BLAKE TREINEN

BOGMAN

Well, I'll say it... if you draft Treinen expecting him to have an ERA and WHIP under one you are outside your mind. The xFIP was 2.42 around Treinen and that is way more reliable and still VERY good. Treinen added the cutter and scrapped the change, leading to this amazing year and while I think he can have continued success I expect him to come back to Earth a bit. I would absolutely be taking Díaz ahead of Treinen if they were going at the same point in the draft. Díaz is going to be closing games for that incredible staff in Queens with reigning Cy Young winner deGrom, Syndergaard, Matz and Wheeler, that has me salivating! The ace in Oakland is Mike Fiers, of course this actually worked in Treinen's favor last year as he came in to some tied game situations and wound up with 9 wins. The problem with drafting Díaz is that he's going around some potential huge difference makers at this point. Carlos Correa, Xander Bogaerts, Eugenio Suárez, Vlad Jr and Gleyber Torres are all going behind Edwin Díaz right now. If Díaz fell down to where Treinen is being drafted around 20ish picks lower I would consider him. To be honest I'm not really excited about where Treinen is going either but I'll take him in the 60-70 round over Díaz. This is like a 3 knockdown rule fight.

EDWIN DÍAZ

THE WELSH

What do you say about the best closer in baseball? Edwin Díaz saved 57 games with a sub-2 ERA (with a lower xFIP, which makes him another FIP beater) and was one of four players who pitched 50 or more innings in 2018 with a 15+ K/9. He was awesome. Maybe the best part about him was the discount you got. He was drafted as maybe the 8th, 10th, or even the 12th closer off the board. This year, you are paying for something between the first and third-best closer, and the early looks are saying as high as a top 50 pick. That is what I cannot stand about the price point of closers. Since closer is such a volatile position, I cannot get down with that high of an investment. I do acknowledge the power of owning the best in the game at a position, but it is not what I want to do. Díaz takes a hit based on the defense behind him, which worries me a little. On the other end though, the Mets improved their bats and they have some great starters who will create a lot of save situations. Treinen did a lot of the same great things as Díaz. He comes at little to no discount. His early NFBC ADP is inside the top 70. There is no doubt in my mind that Díaz is one of the top three closers in baseball. What he did, with few bumps in the road, was awesome. If you pinned me down to pick a closer inside the top 75, or even the top 100, there are only three choices I would give you: Kenley Jansen, Craig Kimbrel and Edwin Díaz. Even with his high cost, he is a no-brainer over Treinen. Edwin Díaz KO over Blake Treinen.

★ ★ ★ WINNER - EDWIN DÍAZ 10-8 ★ ★ ★

20 19 | Judges Scorecard

EDDY ALMAGUER	CHRIS BLESSING	TIM HEANEY
DÍAZ 10-7	DÍAZ 10-9	DÍAZ 10-9

Round 43: Blake Treinen vs Edwin Díaz

SCOOTER GENNETT VS DEE GORDON

	SCOOTER GENNETT			ROUND 44	DEE GORDON		
AVG.	.310	★			AVG.	.268	
HR	23	★			HR	4	
RBI	92	★			RBI	36	
RUNS	86	★			RUNS	62	
SB	4			★	SB	30	

SCOOTER GENNETT

BOGMAN

Dee Gordon is the epitome of a one trick pony, the only thing he does well on a year in and year out basis is steal bases. Most guys that only have the ability to steal bases will at least score a ton of runs on top of it but Gordon has only scored 100 runs once and that was in 2017 when Stanton was driving everyone in. This season Gordon is slated to hit at the bottom of the order (he didn't above 6 after August 9th last season) for the Mariners so run scoring and base stealing opportunities are going to drop. Gordon's career high in HRs is 4, RBI is 46 and he can hit for average as he's hit .333 in a season before but last season he was all the way down to .268 so I wouldn't bank on it. Scooter Gennett won't steal many bases as his career high is 8 but he's hit at least .290 with 80 R, 23 HR, and 92 RBI over the last two seasons. The only thing that Gordon has going for him is that he's going about 20-30 spots below Gennett but there are many other players that will give me SBs that are going in the same range as him that I would much rather have. Early round KO for for Gennett.

DEE GORDON

THE WELSH

The days of the "one-trick pony" fantasy player are moving further into the past. We used to pay a premium for guys like Dee Gordon and Billy Hamilton. We would count on runs from them but give up hope of home runs and RBI. Gordon in 2017 showed us that although he does not have power numbers (and never will), he still posted three elite categories with 114 runs, a .308 batting average and 60 stolen bases. In 2018 Gordon's performance slipped. He had 51 less hits than the previous year (he did play 17 less games) and his average dipped 40 points. The most disturbing trend came in stolen bases. He had half the stolen bases of the previous year in only 17 less games. The worst trend was Gordon pressing. He pulled the ball 3% more than in the previous three seasons, while also putting the ball in the air more. Gordon's ground ball rate was 3% lower than in previous years. For many batters that is a good thing, but not for Dee. He needs to get on base to steal those bases, and his BABIP dropped 50 points. 2018 could show us the path forward with Dee, but it also could have been a blip. If Dee gets back to getting on base, he is going to steal more bases. The runs probably will not equal 2017 if he is in Seattle, but we can expect him to be more aggressive manufacturing runs. Let's say we meet in the middle and Gordon posts a .275 average with 40+ stolen bases. Would that be worth a top 100 pick? If you said yes, be aware he is currently going outside of the top 100. My argument is not about tearing Gennett down, but buying a player who posts 40+ stolen bases with a good batting average. That value outside of the top 100 could be a game changer for your team. Gennett will likely contribute in only three categories as well. Gordon wins 10-9 over Gennett.

★ ★ ★ **WINNER - DEE GORDON 10-9** ★ ★ ★

20 19

Judges Scorecard

IN THIS LEAGUE

MATT MODICA	CLAY LINK	JAKE CIELY
GORDON 10-9	GENNETT KO	GORDON 10-9

Round 44: Scooter Gennett vs Dee Gordon

MITCH HANIGER VS ELOY JIMENEZ

MITCH HANIGER

AVG.	.285	
HR	26	★
RBI	93	★
RUNS	90	★
SB	8	★

ROUND 45

ELOY JIMENEZ *

	AVG.	.337
★	HR	22
	RBI	75
	RUNS	64
	SB	0

2018 MiLB Stats

MITCH HANIGER

BOGMAN

Mitch Haniger is probably the most boring outfielder you can draft because 90 R and RBI, 25ish HR, a handful of SBs and a mid .280s average is not sexy at all. Most were under the impression that Mitch Haniger wouldn't be able to hit .282 again but he improved to .285 and really just kept the same course from 2017 to 2018 and had a very impressive year. I'm not saying that Haniger is flawless because he's not. Haniger hit 10 of his 26 HRs in the first month and the Mariners have lost a significant amount of firepower from the lineup with Cano and Cruz leaving. Eloy Jimenez is expected to come up to the bigs and light the league on fire and I think that is a very real possibility. Jimenez is more talented than Haniger and I'm sure that will show when he is called up, his numbers actually improved from AA to AAA last season. Eloy is even a better deal than Haniger going off the board at about 20-30 spots below him. The reason I'd take Haniger this season is because we don't know when Eloy will get the call. The dude had nothing to prove at the end of last season and the White Sox didn't call him up. Steamer has him for 133 games but if he even has a tweak or threat of injury the White Sox won't call him up. Give me Haniger this year and Jimenez every year beyond 2019!

ELOY JIMENEZ

THE WELSH

Eloy Jimenez is one of the premier prospects in all of baseball. Jimenez hitting .337 any other year would have been the talk of all of minor league baseball. Vladimir Guerrero hovering around .400 for so long stopped that. Eloy is a rare big power-hitter who controls the strike zone. He not only attacks his pitches, but also makes massive contact. At both stops in the minors in 2018 he hit better than .315. In AAA, Jimenez came .001 of OBP short of 300/400/500, slashing 355/399/597. The bottom line is he is one of the league's best young bats and should see the majority of his 2019 playing time in the majors. The problem is his performance is much less certain than Mitch Haniger. Haniger put up one of the quieter productive seasons of 2018. Haniger has now had two seasons of hitting .285 or better and become a solid five-tool option. Steamer puts these two in a similar range across the board, except with an almost 40 point predicted batting average advantage for Eloy. That's right, the rookie. Think about that for a minute. Steamer has Vlad, Jr. at the top of average for 2019, and fellow rookie Eloy at .294. Mitch's production speaks for itself, without the playing time concerns. Eloy is one of several emerging generational talents, with a pedigree like Juan Soto and Ronald Acuña. He might more resemble Soto, as he and Acuña have different skill sets. Questions about Eloy come priced in to his 100-120 ADP, while Mitch will run you a top 85 pick. Eloy gets major playing time 2019, and returns top four round value. 10-9 in favor of Eloy.

★ ★ ★ **WINNER - MITCH HANIGER 10-9** ★ ★ ★

20 19

IN THIS LEAGUE *Judges Scorecard*

STEVE GARDNER	JAMES ANDERSON	ITL ARMY
HANIGER 10-8	JIMENEZ 10-9	HANIGER 10-8 (77%)

Round 45: Mitch Haniger vs Eloy Jimenez

MIKE CLEVINGER VS MILES MIKOLAS

	CLEVINGER		MIKOLAS
WINS	13		18 ★
ERA	3.02		2.83 ★
WHIP	1.155		1.071 ★
K	207 ★		146
IP	200.0		200.2 ★

ROUND 46

MIKE CLEVINGER
BOGMAN

It seems like Mike Clevinger didn't change much and had way more success because his pitch mix stayed the exact same but he changed how he throws his curveball. His Curveball is his 2nd best pitch according to pitch values behind his slider which has always been his best pitch. Miles Mikolas made an incredible return from Japan. Mikolas came back as the same pitcher he was before but way more efficient but he is a much better real life pitcher than fantasy pitcher. Mikolas isn't a strikeout pitcher at all, he was actually 4th from the bottom in K/9 among qualified pitchers last season at 6.55, and if we look at pitchers with at least 100 innings he's 122 of 140. Mikolas did improve his K rate in the 2nd half from 6.26 to 6.95 but Clevinger jumped from 8.70 to 10.27. Clevinger is the clear winner in this one and he's being drafted way ahead of Mikolas as he deserves to be but I don't think Mikolas is a player I will be drafting at all. Mikolas is a pairing player, meaning if you draft someone who is risky or prone to blow ups Mikolas can pair with him to even him out. Wins are finicky and the ERA and WHIP are close enough for an early round KO for Clevinger.

MILES MIKOLAS
THE WELSH

I remember owning multiple shares of Miles Mikolas last year, wondering every month when he would come back to earth. There was not enough belief in Mikolas by the masses to get value for him in trade. As the months passed and I worried he would slip, he just kept producing. Mikolas finished tied for fourth in baseball with 18 wins. His lack of strikeouts was probably the biggest knock against him. The way he countered that weakness was having the 9th-lowest WHIP in baseball with a 1.07. He locked in 200 innings. Of the 13 pitchers to have 200 innings, no one had a lower BB/9 than Mikolas, with a 1.30. That is only 29 total walks in 200.2 innings. Wins are hard to project so the repeatability of that performance will be a major question in 2019. One positive sign was his 2.17 home ERA. Gaining gold glove first baseman Paul Goldschmidt in the infield will help on both sides of the plate. I will be honest, though, regardless of the great numbers, I think it is tough to take a pitcher whose value relies on wins and who contributes so little in strikeouts. His deep ADP made him a huge value. The same can be said about Mike Clevinger's 2018, but with 200+ strikeouts. Neither come at any discount this year. The Indians have consolidated their roster, while the Cards have added championship-level pieces. Clevinger was close to an xFIP of 4 but walked the third-most batters out of 13 pitchers with 200 or more innings. Clevinger is going around pick 65, with Mikolas hovering in the 80s/90s. This battle comes down to the final round, with Mikolas edging out Clevinger on value alone, 10-9.

★ ★ ★ WINNER - MIKE CLEVINGER 10-7 ★ ★ ★

 *Judges Scorecard*

20
19

ALEX CHAMBERLAIN	PAUL SPORER	NICK POLLACK
CLEVINGER 10-9	CLEVINGER 10-8	CLEVINGER KO

Round 46: Mike Clevinger vs Miles Mikolas

TIM ANDERSON VS JURICKSON PROFAR

	TIM ANDERSON		JURICKSON PROFAR
AVG.	.240	★ AVG.	.254
HR	20	HR	20
RBI	64	★ RBI	77
RUNS	77	★ RUNS	82
SB	26 ★	SB	10

ROUND 47

TIM ANDERSON
THE WELSH

Twenty-eight batters had 20 or more stolen bases in 2018. Ten of those batters also put up at least 20 HR. Tim Anderson was one of them. Anderson did a ton of his damage in the first half of the season with 13 home runs and 21 stolen bases. He cooled off in the second half while struggling to hit right handers. Regardless of the slowdown, Anderson saw career highs across the board except for in batting average. Some of those struggles can be attributed to pressing. He dealt with bad luck as his BABIP was around 30 points lower in 2018 than his career average. Even if changes are not on the horizon, we know Tim Anderson's floor is quite high for counting stats. Jurickson Profar is moving into a very solid spot in Oakland, a solid spot in the order, likely to full-time at bats. Profar is not a sure power hitter regardless of the rise in HR/FB rate. Profar moves away from hitter-friendly Arlington, Texas (rated number one in MLB in 2018 in runs park factor at 1.352 and third in home run park factor at 1.273.) Oakland had the third worst park factor for runs at .840 and for home runs at .756. Steamer agrees Profar will regress, predicting a dip to 13 HR/6 SB in 2019. Anderson should top him in both. These two battle it out, but the power punches from TA mean a 10-8 win.

JURICKSON PROFAR
BOGMAN

Two young potential studs in the middle infield! I have seen Anderson go ahead of Profar in some providers and reverse so they will probably be drafted around the same spot when it's all said and done with. The reason I lean towards Profar is because I fear the bottom out with Tim Anderson. His underlying numbers are awful. His SwStr% of 14.1% is reserved for power hitters only, he was 133/140 qualified hitters and the guys below him included Crush, Stanton, Khris Davis, Baez and Gallo. Anderson's OBP was also 133/140 and he improved his BB rate from 2.1% to 5% from 17 to 18. Anderson's Contact% of 73.7% was 117/140, K% was 117/140 at 24.6% and that BB% was was 128/140, you get the picture he's just not a great hitter. Profar was 32nd in Contact%, he's hitting 2nd in the A's lineup AND he'll qualify at SS, 3B, 1B and 2B! Anderson had better HR and SB numbers last season but I'm afraid of him being relegated to a platoon player against lefties as he hit .282 against them and only .224 against righties. If you buy one make it Profar.

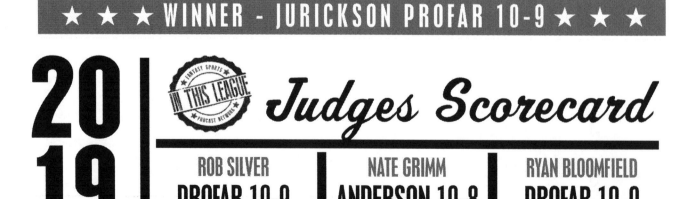

★ ★ ★ ★ WINNER - JURICKSON PROFAR 10-9 ★ ★ ★ ★

20 19

Judges Scorecard

IN THIS LEAGUE

ROB SILVER	NATE GRIMM	RYAN BLOOMFIELD
PROFAR 10-9	ANDERSON 10-8	PROFAR 10-9

Round 47: Tim Anderson vs Jurickson Profar

JESÚS AGUILAR VS MIGUEL CABRERA

	JESÚS AGUILAR		ROUND		MIGUEL CABRERA	
AVG.	.274			★ AVG.	.299	
HR	35 ★		**48**	HR	3	
RBI	108 ★			RBI	22	
RUNS	80 ★			RUNS	17	
SB	0			SB	0	

JESÚS AGUILAR
BOGMAN

It's hard to argue that a player being picked almost 100 picks ahead of another is more valuable but I will attempt to convince you of that here. Basically it boils down to Jesús Aguilar being figured out a little bit in the 2nd half, and the cause could be many different things. The first thing that jumps out to me is that this was Aguilar's first season of being an everyday player, he had 255 more PA in 2018 than he had in 2017 which was his career high before last season. I'll be the first to admit if you are going to invest a top 80 pick in this dude he has to be in better shape and produce down the stretch. Aguilar also had a hamstring tweak late in July which could have factored into the bad second half. Even with that 2nd half Aguilar still was 14th in HRs and 7th in RBI. Imagine if those results if he can keep the pace in the 2nd half in what will be only his 2nd full season. Miggy is a legend and I'm not saying not to take a risk on him at all but this is really a bad 2nd half for Aguilar vs what could be a non existent 2nd half for Cabrera. Miggy is turning 36 in early April and there is no way we can count on him being healthy this season. I like taking both of these guys but if I have to pick one it's the upside of Aguilar against the injury history of a legend like Miggy.

MIGUEL CABRERA
THE WELSH

I wish I could quit Miguel Cabrera, but I cannot. I am very biased when it comes to Miggy. In this case, though, I think the case for Miggy is justified and simple. Jesús Aguilar's first half in 2018 is largely what we are paying for now. I mean, Aguilar hit 24 home runs in that first half. In the second half his average dipped from the .290s to .245 and he hit only 11 home runs. I think with Aguilar I expect a middle ground of 25 home runs, with an average that is somewhere between .245 and .260. Steamer says he will hit .245. Miggy, on the other hand, has struggled with injuries for two years now. While Miggy has maintained many of his contact numbers, held off a drop in HR/FB% and even raised his walk percentage, his power has disappeared. The anti-Miggy camp can cite age, as he will be 36 years old going into May. The pro-Miggy camp can look to injuries to explain the power dip. We can all look at his ISO and see it is 100 points lower in 2018/2017 than it was in 2016, but does that mean it can't rebound? I don't think so. Cabrera showed solid contact while hitting .299 before tearing his bicep tendon last year. That gives me hope we are not done seeing the impact that Miggy has delivered over the years. From a draft perspective, this matchup has a big value difference. Aguilar, to my amazement, is going inside the top 85, while all-but-forgotten Miggy sits in the 160s in NFBC ADP. Do not get me wrong, if Miggy's ADP were closer to 100, the risk would outweigh the reward. At this cost, it is a no-brainer to "gamble" on Miggy's return over Aguilar's 2018 first half. Miggy with a late-round KO.

★ ★ ★ WINNER - JESÚS AGUILAR 10-8 ★ ★ ★

20 19 — In This League — Judges Scorecard

DEREK VAN RIPER	JAKE CIELY	JASON COLLETTE
AGUILAR 10-8	DRAW	AGUILAR 10-8

Round 48: Jesús Aguilar vs Miguel Cabrera

SHOHEI OHTANI VS JOEY GALLO

	SHOHEI OHTANI				JOEY GALLO
AVG.	.285 ★		AVG.		.206
HR	22		★ HR		40
RBI	61		★ RBI		92
RUNS	59		★ RUNS		82
SB	10 ★		SB		3

ROUND 49

SHOHEI OHTANI

BOGMAN

If you listened to our podcast late last season you know I was all aboard the potential of Joey Gallo for 2019 for the month of August. Gallo for whatever reason raised his average for the month above the Mendoza line all the way to the tune of .294. Just imagine the possibility of all that power hitting .294 for a season! But, he shattered my 2019 dream by resuming his status quo in September and dropping his average literally 100 points to .194 for the month. There isn't much point in taking Gallo when you can lose a few HRs and pick up 50 points in average with someone like Encarnacion. What makes this matchup interesting is that Ohtani is coming off TJ surgery and is supposed to be the Angels DH and not pitch at all this season. A season of Ohtani hitting would be incredible as he hit .285 in 367 PA last season and his power was no fluke AND he stole 10 bases. The issue is as of right now there is no hitting plan for him although he is reportedly not going to be ready at the beginning of the season. The other thing we have to look out for is the potential shut down or if there is any tweak of anything how quickly will the Angels bring out the hook. Both players have faults and are going close to each other, give me the upside of Ohtani as a fulltime bat! Too many swings and misses for Gallo to have a puncher's chance.

JOEY GALLO

THE WELSH

This might be one of my favorite debates of the book, because it is totally weird and wild. Shohei Ohtani is only going to be a hitter in 2019, but he does not have a defined everyday role. The assumption is he will get his time at DH, the spot Albert Pujols currently occupies. In formats including OBP as a category, Joey Gallo's value doubles. Gallo's power numbers are the elite of elite, but he is a major liability in batting average. While no month in 2018 was great for Gallo, June and July were particularly bad. Gallo posted a sub-.200 BABIP in that stretch. His second half was more encouraging as he hit .239 with 18 home runs in only 55 games. I want to put something in perspective with Gallo. Steamer projects him with a .225 average for 2019. That would be a career best. They also predict 39 home runs and 94 RBI. Khris Davis projects at .240 (which is hilarious since he has batted exactly .247 for four straight seasons) with 38 home runs and 103 RBI. Davis is sporting a top-45 ADP in NFBC drafts, while Gallo sits just outside the top 100. I am not trying to convince you Gallo is going to have a high batting average in 2019, and it certainly will not be better than Ohtani's. What I am selling is if you are in the market for three above-average categories, Gallo makes as much sense as Khris Davis does. There is little not to like about Ohtani, who has a later ADP than last year since he is just a hitter, but it is impossible to be sure of full-time numbers from him. Gallo takes this matchup 10-8 based on a better guarantee of playing time and massive power numbers.

★ ★ ★ **WINNER - JOEY GALLO 10-9** ★ ★ ★

20 19

IN THIS LEAGUE — *Judges Scorecard*

STEVE GARDNER	KC BUBBA	TIM HEANEY
GALLO 10-9	GALLO 10-9	OHTANI 10-8

DAVID PRICE VS MIKE FOLTYNEWICZ

DAVID PRICE				MIKE FOLTYNEWICZ	
WINS	16 ★	ROUND 50		WINS	13
ERA	3.58		★	ERA	2.85
WHIP	1.142		★	WHIP	1.082
K	177		★	K	202
IP	176.0		★	IP	183.0

DAVID PRICE

THE WELSH

The Folty love this year reminds me a lot of the Clevinger excitement from last draft season. Mike Foltynewicz threw his slider more in 2018 which resulted in higher strikeout numbers. His ERA was under three, though his xFIP showed performance closer to a four ERA. I have a hard time trusting guys with a BB/9 higher than three to repeat their performance. It is not that there is not value, I just find repeatability is hard with high walk rates – if the pitcher's stuff is off for a start, struggles mount quickly. Folty also pitched to the fourth lowest BABIP in baseball in 2018: .251. Perhaps Folty is a pitcher who can consistently suppress BABIP, but I am not a believer -- especially at a top 80 ADP cost. David Price has run into bumps recently, but has a track record of consistency. In the 2018 second half he had a 2.25 ERA, and steps back into 2019 with that momentum on one of baseball's best teams. Price's cost is currently at least a round later than Folty, which makes for a deal. Even if compared one to one without looking at ADP, David Price represents the ceiling and floor I am drafting rather than the regression I expect with Folty. 10-7 Price with the win.

MIKE FOLTYNEWICZ

BOGMAN

Everyone has been waiting for Folty to break out since he was first round pick in 2010 and it finally happened! He was toiling around in the bigs with Atlanta since 2015 and nothing really seemed to work until he started throwing his slider way more last year. Everything clicked, the ERA dropped almost 2 runs from 4.79 to 2.85, WHIP fell from 1.48 to 1.08, K/9 rose, BB/9 dropped and he struck out 200 batters! David Price also made an adjustment, he stopped playing Fortnite and his ERA dropped from 4.42 in the 1st half to 2.25 in the 2nd half! Some of the underlying stats are in Folty's favor including GB%, HR/FB, xFIP and Contact%. David Price had a ton of QS though and does have the edge in experience and is on a great team in terms of getting wins in Boston. I'm going to let my curiosity get the better of me here and take Folty to see if he can improve on his first great season. An offseason of watching film and tinkering with what worked last year could really vault him into the upper echelon of pitchers in 2019. I'm not against doubling up and taking both of these guys because Price is coming at what I would consider a deal about 20-30 spots below Folty. Give me Folty by the narrowest of margins in the cards!

★ ★ ★ WINNER - DAVID PRICE 10-7 ★ ★ ★

2019 Judges Scorecard

IN THIS LEAGUE

ENO SARRIS	PAUL SPORER	JASON COLLETTE
PRICE KO	PRICE 10-7	PRICE 10-9

Round 50: David Price vs Mike Foltynewicz

DAVID PERALTA VS AARON HICKS

			ROUND 51			
AVG.	.285			★	AVG.	.337
HR	26 ★				HR	22
RBI	93 ★				RBI	75
RUNS	90 ★				RUNS	64
SB	8 ★				SB	0

DAVID PERALTA

THE WELSH

David Peralta loves Arizona. It is fair to say Arizona also loves Peralta, especially for his .341 batting average at home in 2018. Peralta struggled against lefties with a .237 average, although he still hit .291 against lefties at home. If you were to take him out of Arizona, there could be issues. Guess what -- not only is Peralta not gone, he is hitting third in the new Diamondback lineup. He has now hit .293 overall for two straight seasons, so we can feel comfortable with Peralta's contributions to the batting average category. His power numbers were a bit inflated in 2018 as he nearly doubled his HR/FB rate from 2017. I will be the first to admit that ratio should come down. Even if you were to remove some of Peralta's power, though, he is still in line for a major RBI bump this year, which given his average could push his career high. Aaron Hicks finally got his shot in 2018, and proved to be able to put up some serious stats. I question how committed the Yankees are to Hicks, especially as rumors of big free agent signings and trades continue to circle. Were the Yankees to shake up the roster, he would be one of the most likely players to be effected. In the 5x5 format, let's call HR/RBI/runs a wash between the two. You're looking at a five to six stolen base difference in favor of Hicks or a 40 to 50 points batting average difference in favor of Peralta. Once you throw on top that Peralta is going 10-15 spots lower, Peralta gets the KO.

AARON HICKS

BOGMAN

I don't think that there's any doubt that Peralta is the better player in this debate. This is the rare circumstance where the better player isn't the pick because Hicks has way more around him than Peralta does. Peralta is the better hitter here without a doubt the batting average will show that (career .293 for Peralta vs career .236 for Hicks) David Peralta also was 2nd in the league among qualified hitters in hard contact% at 48.6% behind only Matt Carpenter. However, the contact% was almost identical last season at 78.2% to 78%. The Peralta problem is that the DBacks lost Goldy and Pollock at the top of the lineup so Peralta is missing some firepower around him while Hicks is sandwiched between Aaron Judge and Giancarlo Stanton. If we're breaking it down by the 5 categories Peralta gets average and probably HR with that Hard Contact%, Hicks is going to win SBs and Runs for sure and I think he will have more RBI opportunities as well. They are going within 5 picks of each other so far, I'll take the one with the better value in your draft but I lean on the lineup when almost everything else is close and Hicks' lineup is better. To the cards in this one with Hicks as the victor.

★ ★ ★ WINNER - DAVID PERALTA 10-9 ★ ★ ★

2019 | Judges Scorecard

CLAY LINK	RYAN BLOOMFIELD	CHRIS MEANEY
PERALTA 10-8	PERALTA 10-8	HICKS 10-9

Round 51: David Peralta vs Aaron Hicks

MICHAEL CONFORTO ~~VS~~ EDDIE ROSARIO

MICHAEL CONFORTO			ROUND 52		EDDIE ROSARIO
AVG.	.243			★ AVG.	.288
HR	28 ★			HR	24
RBI	82 ★			RBI	77
RUNS	78			★ RUNS	87
SB	3			★ SB	8

MICHAEL CONFORTO   THE WELSH

It was a tale of two halves with these two. Michael Conforto had a miserable .216 start but still managed 11 home runs. He turned it around in the second half with a .273 average and 16 more home runs. Eddie Rosario did the opposite: a .311 first half average along with 19 home runs followed by hitting.240 and only 5 home runs in the second half. One interesting note: last year Conforto hit under .240 both from the number three and the number four spots in the lineup. From the number five spot, he hit .347 in 20 games. Roster Resource has Conforto hitting five this year behind some solid contact bats in Wilson Ramos, Robinson Canó and Jed Lowrie. I look at the end of both players' seasons, the improved lineup around Conforto, similar production outside of average and if you give me two rounds of draft value, Conforto is a clear choice. I think Conforto sets a new career high in at least two of his 5x5 stats in 2019. Conforto with a tight 10-9 victory.

EDDIE ROSARIO   BOGMAN

Eddie Rosario was well on his way to crushing his 2017 numbers when a shoulder injury sapped his power in late June and a quad injury shut him down for good in September. In fact until the shoulder soreness Rosario was hitting .321 and was crushing Conforto. Conforto did come through with a really big 2nd half hitting 17 of his 28 bombs in the 2nd half with his average ballooning from .216 to .273. So we have a first half player and a second half player here. Eddie Rosario is going about 20 picks ahead of Conforto as I'm typing this but I don't think that's going to last as the Conforto hype machine takes over. The underlying numbers don't help too much in this one either, they both are all over the place in contact numbers, Rosario has the better K% but worse BB% and they both were right around their career BABIP. I think they both have very high ceilings and pretty high floors as well so I guess the fact that Rosario has been consistent two years in a row and was so good before the shoulder injury has me leaning slightly his way. The Twins also added some firepower behind him and in front of him with Nelson Cruz and CJ Cron. Hicks in the tightest of score card races!

★ ★ ★ WINNER - EDDIE ROSARIO 10-9 ★ ★ ★

2019

Judges Scorecard

JOE PISAPIA	JAKE CIELY	TIM HEANEY
ROSARIO 10-8	ROSARIO 10-9	CONFORTO 10-9

Round 52: Michael Conforto vs Eddie Rosario

JOSÉ PERAZA VS JONATHAN VILLAR

	JOSÉ PERAZA				JONATHAN VILLAR	
AVG.	.288	★	ROUND	AVG.	.260	
HR	14	★	53	HR	14	
RBI	58	★		RBI	46	
RUNS	85	★		RUNS	54	
SB	23		★	SB	35	

JOSÉ PERAZA

BOGMAN

I don't know that this one should really be a debate, the only thing that makes it close is Villar has a chance to steal a ton of bases. That is by no way a guarantee though as he dropped from 62 to 23 and then was back up to 35. Villar is also slated to hit 3rd in the horrible Orioles lineup and his SBs fell off when he wasn't hitting one or two in the lineup (21 at 1 or 2, 14 at 3rd or lower). Peraza hits at the top of the much improved Reds lineup and he's no slouch on the basepaths either stealing at least 20 bases the last 3 seasons. Peraza doesn't have to have a ton of power because he's one of the best pure hitters in the league, 10th in hits at 182, 9th in contact% at 87.7% and 2nd behind Brantley in z-Contact% at 95.7%. Peraza hitting at the top of the lineup will run into HRs and RBI with his contact rate being so high. Villar is not a contact hitter he was 128/140 in contact% and 138/140 in z-contact%. This isn't really a debate, Villar is the better hitter, hits in the better lineup and taking Villar is just chasing SBs. Peraza in an early KO here!

JONATHAN VILLAR

THE WELSH

If we tried to make graphs of fantasy player approval rating, fantasy production, or even ADP for Jonathan Villar's last three years, they would be all over the place. While Villar's 19 home run 62 stolen base 2016 is a distant memory, we got a flash in the second half of last year of what could make Villar special. Before being traded from the Brewers to the Orioles, Villar hit six home runs and stole 14 bases in 85 games. In 54 games after being traded to Baltimore, Villar hit eight homers and, more importantly, stole 21 bases. Baltimore unleashed Villar on the basepaths. Villar also hit the ball in the air more often, which resulted in his uptick in power. That is key to Villar's value: actual power numbers to go with the speed. Villar has hit double-digit home runs three straight years and averaged 40 stolen bases per year over that time period. José Peraza has never had more than 23 stolen bases in a season (barely more than Villar's hot 2018 stretch run). Peraza strength has been hitting. While Peraza has been one of the top contact guys in baseball, he only posted a .288 average last year. He hit a career-high 14 home runs, and that came on a career high 6.8% HR/FB. His game is not built around power. Runs and RBI may be a wash between these two players. Peraza is better in average, while Villar clearly has home runs and stolen bases. They are going next to each other in drafts, so neither is coming at a better value. Baltimore gave us insight into what they are willing to do with Villar, and it could be of huge benefit to fantasy owners. Villar with the 10-8 due to better counting stats.

★ ★ ★ ★ WINNER - JONATHAN VILLAR 10-9 ★ ★ ★ ★

20 19 | *Judges Scorecard*

IN THIS LEAGUE — FANTASY SPORTS — PODCAST NETWORK

DEREK VAN RIPER	SAMMY REID	NATE GRIMM
PERAZA 10-9	VILLAR 10-9	VILLAR 10-9

ROBBIE RAY vs JOSÉ BERRIOS

ROBBIE RAY			ROUND	JOSÉ BERRIOS		
WINS	6			★ WINS	12	
ERA	3.93		**54**	★ ERA	3.84	
WHIP	1.350			★ WHIP	1.144	
K	165			★ K	202	
IP	123.2			★ IP	192.1	

ROBBIE RAY
THE WELSH

A straight one-on-one matchup here does not seem close. José Berrios has seen a three-year improvement in strikeouts, K/9, BB/9 and ERA. Ray had a rough 2018, pushing through injuries for 123 innings. As usual, Ray was an absolute stud in strikeouts with a 12.01 K/9. That was fifth-best among pitchers with over 120 innings. Unfortunately, those 165 strikeouts came with an awful 5.09 BB/9. That was the worst among 2018 pitchers with 120 innings or more. Like I said, a one-on-one comparison between these two pitchers is tough. The 'Ray of light' (I hate myself) for Robbie came with his second half, where he had a 3.23 ERA (almost two runs less than the first half). Meanwhile, Berrios regressed a bit in the second half, going from a 3.68 ERA to 4.15. Ray had more strikeouts, fewer hits allowed and even a better WHIP. Ray had a 1.49 first half WHIP, no surprise with those bad walk numbers, but he dropped it to 1.26 in the second half. Berrios went from a 1.01 first half WHIP to 1.40 in the second half. Ray was so popular coming into 2018 that many owners may feel they were burned by him. If you look at it objectively, though, you can see he regained form after recovering from first-half injuries. Here is the final great selling point: Ray is going 40 or more picks after Berrios. I am not saying Berrios is not worth a pick between #70 and #80 overall. I'd probably take Berrios at that value, but Ray's 2019 rebound if you can take him after pick 110 will be an even better value. While this is a close, hard-fought match, I will take Ray 10-9.

JOSÉ BERRIOS
BOGMAN

Berrios keeps getting better year after year and 2018 was no different. Berrios improved his ERA, WHIP, K/9, BB/9, xFIP, BABIP, FB/HR and SwStr% in 2018. I don't see why Berrios won't improve this season, last year was his first with a full slate of starts and now it's all just tweaking to get better. Both of these guys had weird splits last season, Berrios was great at home (2.41 ERA) and awful on the road (5.17 ERA) and also better in the 1st half (3.53 ERA) than in the 2ns half (4.24 ERA). Robbie Ray was better in the 2nd half (3.23 ERA) than in the 1st half (5.03) and was much better on the road (3.05 ERA) than at home even with AZ installing the humidor (3.05 ERA). Ray getting better in the 2nd half of last season is no surprise as he was recovering from an abdominal issue for a big chunk of the season. This one is close with the weird splits and Robbie Ray has been involved in some trade rumors. The deciding factor here is the BB/9 rate, Berrios is only walking 2.85 per 9 innings while Robbie Ray has increased his walk rate every year and last year it climbed to over 5. Give me the improving young buck over the vet who probably peaked in 2017.

★ ★ ★ **WINNER - JOSÉ BERRIOS 10-8** ★ ★ ★

20 19 | Judges Scorecard

PAUL SPORER	ALEX CHAMBERLAIN	NICK POLLACK
BERRIOS KO	**DRAW**	**BERRIOS 10-9**

Round 54: Robbie Ray vs José Berrios

JUSTIN TURNER VS ROUGNED ODOR

	JUSTIN TURNER				ROUGNED ODOR
AVG.	.312 ★		AVG.		.253
HR	14		★ HR		18
RBI	52	ROUND 55	★ RBI		63
RUNS	62		★ RUNS		76
SB	2		★ SB		12

JUSTIN TURNER

THE WELSH

.356 -- that was Justin Turner batting average in the second half of 2018. Wow. That was 100 points higher than Turner's first half average. Turner had another injury-plagued season in 2018, and his early wrist injury led to those splits. He has long been a trustworthy source of batting average. Since coming to the Dodgers, Turner has only hit lower than .290 once. I also like Odor. I was firm in believing Odor would have a boost in average in 2018, which he did. Odor's batting average boost looks to be a change in philosophy that could also result in a dip in power. He swung 4% less often at pitches outside of the zone while making 3% more overall contact. His HR/FB rate dropped by about 3% compared to previous years. Odor's power numbers are no longer guaranteed to beat Turner's. Odor's only clear advantage now is in stolen bases, but it comes at a significant cost to batting average. I prefer Turner because he is not someone you have to build a strategy around. If you take Odor, you will have to account for damage to your batting average that could greatly alter your team strategy. Unless Odor returns to his 2016 form, Turner scores the 10-9 win.

ROUGNED ODOR

BOGMAN

I've mentioned it before that sometimes we can go overboard on the underlying/analytical stats and dive too deep there when the 5 categories are what we are really looking for. This is easily one of those debates as Justin Turner is clearly the better hitter between these two. Turner is a great contact% hitter, he beat Odor by almost 60 points in average last year and he would have been 6th in contact% if he had qualified. Turner didn't qualify though because he was only able to play in 103 games last season as missing games has been the signature of his career. Turner has played in 125 or more games only 3 times in his 10 year MLB career. Last season Turner dealt with wrist, hip and groin injuries. Odor has played in at least 120 games the last 4 seasons but he dealt with a quad injury pretty much all season last year but missed the majority of his games in the first month. The one hit tool Odor has over Turner is power as he's hit 30 HRs twice in his 5 seasons whereas Turner has never hit 30 and only gone over 20 twice in his career. Odor is going 20 spots later than Turner, has a much better injury history and has outperformed Turner in everything except batting average 2 years in a row and 3 out of 5 categories 3 years in a row. More power, more speed, cheaper cost is an easy early round KO for Odor. Ask Joey Bats how deadly that right hook is!

★ ★ ★ **WINNER - JUSTIN TURNER 10-8** ★ ★ ★

20 19

Judges Scorecard

ROB SILVER	MATT MODICA	JAMES ANDERSON
TURNER 10-7	TURNER 10-8	TURNER 10-9

Round 55: Rougned Odor vs Justin Turner

DANIEL MURPHY VS NELSON CRUZ

	DANIEL MURPHY		ROUND 56		NELSON CRUZ	
AVG.	.299	★			AVG.	.256
HR	12			★	HR	37
RBI	42			★	RBI	97
RUNS	40			★	RUNS	70
SB	3	★			SB	1

DANIEL MURPHY

THE WELSH

It is a fantasy dream when any hitter goes to Colorado. A high-contact hitter like Daniel Murphy going to Coors Field is even more exciting. Prior to 2018, Murphy was a 24 HR/90 Run/90 RBI/.300 average hitter for two seasons. Injuries slowed the first half of Murphy's 2018. In the final 63 games of 2018, Murphy hit .315 with 11 HR. Though he will play first base for Colorado, he will still qualify at second base. Nelson Cruz hit .218 at home and .295 on the road in 2018. Cruz is coming off a less-than-stellar second half, hitting only .242 while seeing his strikeout rate rise by 2.5%. It is difficult to gauge if the wheels are about to come off for the veteran Cruz, especially with a new landing spot in Minnesota. Truth be told, either Cruz or Murphy would be a great post-100 draft target. Murphy, who was very recently a top 50 pick, is going in the pick 100-120 range. Cruz is sitting in the pick 90-100 range. You get a premium position and better draft value with Murphy, or get more HR and RBI with Cruz. Take position, value and Coors with Murphy: a 10-8 win.

NELSON CRUZ

BOGMAN

This one is going to be all about value. If we look at the ADPs of these two players right now Cruz is actually ahead of Murphy but if we look at drafts after Murphy signed with the Rockies he wins by at least a round and a half. I have to admit when Murphy signed with the Rockies I was really excited, a great average hitter going to the thin air of Colorado AND wedged between Charlie Blackmon and Nolan Arenado is sexy! What isn't sexy is missing 71 games last season with a knee injury that has bothered him for awhile. In the past 5 seasons here are the floor numbers for Nelson Cruz, 144 games played, .256 average, 70 runs, 37 HR and 93 RBI. 144 games played would be the most over the last 5 seasons for Daniel Murphy. In fact over the last 4 seasons outside of batting average and SBs (which are negligible since the high between them is 5) Murphy has only beaten Cruz in runs once in 2017 by 3, all other categories go to Cruz. Even at age 38 Cruz is a safer choice over Daniel Murphy. Murphy has the higher ceiling but much lower floor as well. The closer we get to the season the higher Murphy is going to go, give me Cruz in a split judges decision.

★ ★ ★ WINNER - DANIEL MURPHY 10-9 ★ ★ ★

2019

Judges Scorecard

STEVE GARDNER	JASON COLLETTE	JAKE CIELY
MURPHY 10-9	MURPHY 10-9	CRUZ 10-9

Round 56: Daniel Murphy vs Nelson Cruz

YU DARVISH VS MASAHIRO TANAKA

DARVISH			ROUND 57		MASAHIRO TANAKA	
WINS	1			★	WINS	12
ERA	4.95			★	ERA	3.75
WHIP	1.425			★	WHIP	1.128
K	49			★	K	159
IP	40.0			★	IP	156.0

YU DARVISH

BOGMAN

Boy did I look like a silly goose last year owning all of the Darvish shares! Darvish had elbow and triceps issues that held him to only 40 innings over 8 starts last season and elbow surgery in September. The procedure for Darvish was debridement which is not very invasive and he started his throwing program in mid December with the expectation that he will be back for Opening Day. Tanaka missed 5 starts with a hamstring issue last year but the elbow issues he has gone through are a thing of the past. Tanaka has weird underlying numbers, his xFIP was within .02 the last 2 seasons at a 3.43 average but his ERA was almost a run lower in 18. Tanaka also had a top 10 SwStr% but his K/9 was under the top 25 because he pitches to contact. Only deGrom, Corbin and Tanaka were top 10 in SwStr% and top 25 in GB/FB which is very impressive. Tanaka is very, very safe and to be honest I'm not against taking him and then Darvish. Upside is the name of the game for Darvish, he's gone over 200 Ks 3 times in his 6 MLB seasons and he's had a K/9 over 10 every single season he's pitched. Darvish is available and the best price of his career going around pick 150 and we need to pounce. Darvish upside wins this one in the cards.

MASAHIRO TANAKA

THE WELSH

Yu Darvish's 2018 right elbow arthroscopic surgery raises serious concerns for his health going forward. Darvish is expected back in time for Spring Training, after throwing for the first time back post-surgery in mid-January. Darvish's injuries are a serious concern. Masahiro Tanaka, on the other hand, has seemingly teetered on the edge of major injury for several years. After a disappointing first half, Tanaka's second half 2.85 ERA was an improvement of two full runs while his K/9 went up to around 9 ½ and his BB/9 dropped to 1.61. The addition of more bullpen arms in New York makes me higher on Tanaka for 2019. I know the possibility of shorter starts sounds counterproductive for a starting pitcher. We want our starters to go deep and rack up strikeouts. Tanaka last year through his first two turns in the batting order had a 27% strikeout percentage and kept batters at or under a .230 batting average. Once he got to the third time through the order, though, his strikeout percentage dropped to 16.9% and opposing batters hit .290 against him. Maybe shortening Tanaka's outings will reduce his counting stats, but lower innings could help him maintain higher quality performance. Tanaka might be one of the best starting pitchers you can draft after pick 125, and he is a no-brainer over Darvish coming off the injury. Tanaka with the KO.

★ ★ ★ **WINNER - YU DARVISH 10-9** ★ ★ ★

20 19

IN THIS LEAGUE *FANTASY SPORTS* *PODCAST NETWORK*

Judges Scorecard

EDDY ALMAGUER	NATE GRIMM	ENO SARRIS
DARVISH 10-9	**TANAKA 10-7**	**DARVISH 10-8**

Round 57: Yu Darvish vs Masahiro Tanaka

DAVID DAHL VS ANDREW MCCUTCHEN

	DAVID DAHL			ANDREW MCCUTCHEN
AVG.	.273 ★	ROUND 58	AVG.	.255
HR	16		★ HR	20
RBI	48		★ RBI	65
RUNS	31		★ RUNS	83
SB	5		★ SB	14

DAVID DAHL   THE WELSH

If you know me, you know I am not a big David Dahl guy -- which makes doing the deep dive on him all the more interesting. Dahl has not played much in part because he has been a walking medical ward of injuries, though to be fair he has also been blocked positionally when healthy. He finally got some run in 2018 and was actually pretty consistent. In his last 24 games starting September 1, Dahl hit .287 with 9 HOUR and 27 RBI. Momentum is firmly on his side coming into 2019. Even though I am writing him up, I am cautious of Dahl's likely high cost. Many are valuing Dahl as a top 70 player. While Dahl's strong finish supports optimism, I am concerned by his season-long .200 average on the road while running up a .326 average in Colorado. Luckily, he will again play half his games in Colorado, so it is fair to take that production into account when predicting this year. Andrew McCutchen moves to Philly, which is a positive landing spot for offense. McCutchen's ceiling is limited, but a 25 HR/80 Run/80 RBI season would help anyone's team. Better, he is around 150 in NFBC ADP. Steamer favors McCutchen over Dahl in all categories except for batting average, partly because they only project Dahl to play 116 games. That is the problem, folks! If Dahl plays 150 games, he is probably going to take at worst three of the 5X5 categories, but there is no guarantee he will stay healthy. I hate Dahl's cost, and I cannot stress that enough. Here is the case for Dahl: he is a hitter coming off that hot final stretch, trending up, and playing in Colorado. That has to be valued over the guy who is aging out of baseball, regardless of McCutcheon's value. This is an absolute slugfest that comes down to the wire. It is even until our third judge (who lives in Colorado) swings it to Dahl. 10-9 victory.

ANDREW MCCUTCHEN   BOGMAN

No one understands the David Dahl hype more than I do. I've owned him in a dynasty league for what seems like forever and a day at this point. Dahl is a high end prospect with power and speed plus the benefit of hitting in Coors AND he hit 9 HRs in the last month last season. It's no surprise that he is being draft in the top 100 right now. Dahl is just too injury prone to be taking a big risk on, his inside injuries page is longer than a George RR Martin novel and McCutchen has played at least 146 games every year since 2010. Cutch won't be winning another MVP or anything but he is fairly consistent, 20ish HRs, 10ish swipes and about 80 RBI and runs. The only thing that has been up and down for McCutchen is his batting average, it's been anywhere from .314 to .255 over the last 3 seasons. McCutchen's underlying stats are almost all better than Dahl's as well including Contact%, SwStr%, Hard Contact%, K% and BB%. I understand wanting a young stud cleanup hitter in Colorado but McCutchen is not only the more valuable pick I would bet that he ends up being higher ranked at the end of the season even if it's only because he plays more games. Let someone else take Dahl and watch him gas out in the mid rounds!

★ ★ ★ WINNER - DAVID DAHL 10-8 ★ ★ ★

20 19 | Judges Scorecard

CHRIS BLESSING	PAUL SPORER	RYAN BLOOMFIELD
DAHL 10-7	DAHL 10-9	MCCUTCHEN 10-8

Round 58: David Dahl vs Andrew McCutchen

KYLE FREELAND VS KEVIN GAUSMAN

	KYLE FREELAND		ROUND 59		KEVIN GAUSMAN
WINS	17 ★			WINS	10
ERA	2.85 ★			ERA	3.92
WHIP	1.245 ★			WHIP	1.301
K	173 ★			K	148
IP	202.1 ★			IP	183.2

KYLE FREELAND

BOGMAN

Freeland looks like a pitcher that is set to get a dose of reality in 2019. He pitches in Coors Field, had an xFip almost a run and a half higher than his ERA and had an incredible 17 wins which was tied for 7th most in the bigs. I don't think this was as much of fluke as people think though, he pitches well to contact being top 30 in soft contact% among pitchers with at least 100 IP and he is top 10 in HR/FB despite playing in homer happy Coors Field. The splits were also in Freeland's favor as he pitched to a better ERA at home than on the road (2.40 to 3.23) and he got better in the 2nd half (3.11 down to 2.49). Gausman also saw great improvement in 2018 after being moved to the Braves. The NL seems to suite Gausman better as he lowered his ERA from 4.43 in his first 21 starts to 2.87 in his 10 Atlanta starts. Gausman was helped out by a better defense for sure, like Freeland he isn't a dominate strikeout pitcher he's more of a pitch to contact guy. The reason Freeland is being drafted ahead of Gausman is because Gausman has seen his ERA balloon up over 4 in 3 of his 6 seasons, he's not exactly trustworthy. Tack on the fact that the Braves have 9 pitchers that can fill 3 spots means that early season success is imperative to Gausman keeping his job. Freeland has the slightest of edges in the cards here.

KEVIN GAUSMAN

THE WELSH

In 2018, fewer people needed a change of scenery more than Kevin Gausman. Through 124 innings in Baltimore he had a 4.43 ERA and 1.379 WHIP while allowing 10.1 hits per nine innings. The trade to Atlanta did wonders, as he improved to a 2.87 ERA, 1.14 WHIP, and 7.5 hits per nine. Gausman's 3.78 FIP as a Brave better represents how he pitched than his amazing ERA does, while still being a full run better than his awful ERA as an Oriole. I just cannot decide what to think of Freeland. Freeland had a 2.85 ERA overall with a 2.40 ERA in Colorado. His 3.67 FIP was similar to Gausman's. Neither are great strikeout pitchers, while Freeland walks more batters. Steamer is not high on either for 2019. Gausman is projected to post a 4.15 ERA, close to his 2018 xFIP of 4.19. Steamer projects Freeland's ERA will rise to 4.62. Steamer has little belief that Freeland's 2018 home ERA is sustainable, and I agree. As neither is an attractive strikeout option I cannot give either the benefit of the doubt. Gausman is going around 60 picks after Freeland in early 2019 drafts. There is no way I would pay for a low-strikeout pitcher in Colorado when I can get the same guy cheaper in Atlanta. This is an easy KO for Gausman on value alone, but even if they were picked at the same spot in drafts I would prefer Gausman.

★ ★ ★ WINNER - KEVIN GAUSMAN 10-9 ★ ★ ★

2019 Judges Scorecard

CLAY LINK	SAMMY REID	JAKE CIELY
FREELAND 10-8	GAUSMAN 10-7	DRAW

Round 59: Kyle Freeland vs Kevin Gausman

EDUARDO RODRIGUEZ

VS

LUIS CASTILLO

	EDUARDO RODRIGUEZ		ROUND 60		LUIS CASTILLO	
WINS	13 ★			WINS	10	
ERA	3.82 ★			ERA	4.30	
WHIP	1.265			★ WHIP	1.220	
K	146			★ K	165	
IP	129.2			★ IP	169.2	

EDUARDO RODRÍGUEZ

BOGMAN

These guys both have a lot to prove in 2019. Luis Castillo was among the most disappointing starters in 2018, a great example of why in most cases we don't take upside over consistency. After an impressive 15 starts in 2017 Castillo came back to Earth over his 31 starts last year. The whole season was inconsistent he was good and then terrible every other month, his ERA fluctuations were 7.85, 3.48, 6.75, 2.25, 5.57, 1.09. Not to be outdone ERod sprained his ankle after his last start before the break right when he seemed to be hitting his stride. When Rodríguez came back he wasn't as effective and was sent to the bullpen to finish out the season. So both were maddening and this season seems to be their best shot to plant a flag in their respected rotations and stay there. I'll lean on Rodríguez in his shot here, he's going about 20 spots after Castillo, his K/9 was right at 10 in his starts and he has a better shot at wins playing for the World Champs. Let someone else reach on Castillo and know that you can take Eduardo later with similar production and they both have the same type of downside. One of the closer ones so far but ERod in a split decision.

LUIS CASTILLO

THE WELSH

Was there a bigger disappointment for fantasy owners last year than Luis Castillo? If he was not the worst, he was certainly close. After a solid rookie season where Castillo had a 3.12 ERA and almost 10 K/9, 2018 saw Castillo's ERA rise to 4.30 and K/9 drop below 9. His season was a tale of two halves. Castillo had a 5.49 first half ERA, then dropped his ERA three full runs to 2.44 in the second half. Castillo added a full strikeout per nine in the second half while posting an elite walk rate of 1.9BB/9. The biggest warning sign was how well opponents hit against him. Castillo suffered the 9th-worst hard hit rate in the majors and the second worst HR/FB ratio (17.9 -- only Jon Gray's 18.1% was worse.) I wish I could get the same draft discount on Castillo players are getting on Eduardo Rodríguez. It is not often you can draft a sub-four ERA and 10 K/9 after pick 140 like you can with Rodríguez. Castillo's ups and downs have made him a great 'post-hype-kinda-hyped-again' sleeper. This debate for me is what this book is all about. I think 9 out of 10 owners would say they would rather have Castillo, but when we look deeper, you see how close this debate really is. You should draft for value in Eduardo, but do not be surprised to see a great improvement from Castillo. 10-9 victory LC.

★ ★ ★ **WINNER - LUIS CASTILLO KO** ★ ★ ★

20 19

Judges Scorecard

NICK POLLACK	ENO SARRIS	ITL ARMY
CASTILLO KO	RODRÍGUEZ 10-8	CASTILLO KO (84%)

Round 60: Eduardo Rodríguez vs Luis Castillo

MAX MUNCY VS NICK CASTELLANOS

	MAX MUNCY			ROUND 61			NICK CASTELLANOS
AVG.	.263	★				AVG.	.298
HR	35	★				HR	23
RBI	79				★	RBI	89
RUNS	75				★	RUNS	88
SB	3	★				SB	2

MAX MUNCY

BOGMAN

Somehow Muncy became 'my guy' last year. I'm guessing it was because I picked him up in a lot of leagues and I was onboard early in the process. This was another example of a guy coming over from another organization and getting his career straightened out by the Dodgers just like we saw with Chris Taylor in 2017. Muncy actually had fewer than 250 big league ABs coming into this season and he was pressed into action with injuries to Turner and Seager early in the season. Muncy was so good that he pushed Bellinger to the OF and played a lot of games at 1st after Turner returned to the lineup. This season he will be the Dodgers starting 2nd baseman and will have 1B and 3B qualifications too. While Muncy did have a bit of a second half backslide his ISO was still over .300 in the 2nd half which was 9th overall behind only Yelich, Trout, Khris Davis, Gallo, O'Hearn, Hoskins, Ohtani and Acuna. I don't really have anything bad to say about Castellanos, he's consistent, hits in the middle of the lineup and is everything we expected him to be. I just like Muncy for the value, he's going about 24 picks after Castellanos and has more power in a better lineup. Muncy for the value but I'm not against pairing these guys as you will be able to play Muncy at 3 different positions.

NICK CASTELLANOS

THE WELSH

I don't give Castellanos enough credit, he's almost like the AL Eugenio Suárez in how he gets overlooked. Castellanos is just one of those guys that feels boring to many people, but his production just isn't boring. His career high average of .298 last year came with a solid BABIP boost, so I'd expect it to come down, but he's still a career .274 hitter, compared to Muncy's .268 from last year. I don't think, Castellanos is a massive ceiling guy, where I am expecting breakout numbers, but the previous two years he's essentially been a 25 home run, 80 run and 90 RBI guy. Muncy, on the other hand, was the big breakout guy in 2018. He blasted 35 home runs and took over a starting role in Los Angeles that no one expected. Muncy had an absurd 29.4% HR/FB rate which was third highest in baseball. In my best Lumberg voice, "Yeah, we're gonna need you to come back to life, thanks." One thing to keep on eye out for is where he is in the lineup, which could have a small effect, possibly on pitches he sees, as last year he played 34 games hitting from the two hole, but hit 16 of his homers from that spot in that time span. Roster resource currently slots him in at the five spot in the lineup. Muncy has the power advantage, where Castellanos has the average to go along with a solid track record. Muncy comes at a slight discount, but don't sleep on Castellanos... again! Nicholas is not the strongest boy in the world, but he is the winner 10-8.

★ ★ ★ WINNER - NICK CASTELLANOS 10-8 ★ ★ ★

2019 | *Judges Scorecard*

JOE PISAPIA	JASON COLLETTE	STEVE GARDNER
CASTELLANOS 10-8	MUNCY 10-9	CASTELLANOS 10-8

TRAVIS SHAW VS ROBINSON CANO

	TRAVIS SHAW		ROUND		ROBINSON CANO	
AVG.	.241			★	AVG.	.303
HR	32 ★		62		HR	10
RBI	86 ★				RBI	50
RUNS	73 ★				RUNS	44
SB	5 ★				SB	0

TRAVIS SHAW

THE WELSH

The two years with the Brewers we've had out of Shaw have built a solid understanding of the player we are investing in. 30+ HR and a 85/85 RUN/RBI range. He raised his walk % by 4% and lowered his strikeout rate by 4% dipping below 20%. He's also had an ISO within .01 over the last two years, .240 and .239, that we completely needed to be sold on his power maintaining, but we can. The defining characteristic for me is where the average sits. He dropped from .273 the previous year to .241 last year. His BABIP is all over the board though. The .273 one could see dropping as he hit a career high .312 BABIP the year before, about 30 points higher than his average. This past year though, he had the leagues 7th lowest BABIP at .242. If we meet in the middle, we have a .255 hitter with 30+ home run power. What I really like about this, is the around 100 ADP on a power very comparable to Khris Davis who costs half the price. Robinson Cano's game was starting to flip to less power prior to him getting caught for being a cheating cheater. The three year decline in HR/FB is a telling sign. I think there are some productive season's still in Canó's future, but it has to come with new expectations that this isn't old Canó. He's going around 130 overall which is a solid value, but I Shaw is a no brainer in a 10-7 win.

ROBINSON CANÓ

BOGMAN

Well I was right and wrong on Shaw going into 2018. I really didn't buy into his great 2017 but he kept the power but was worse in the other 4 categories. He did however play enough games to qualify at 2B and that's why these two are being debated. Surprisingly these two were pretty close in Contact% and had the exact same SwStr% however Canó did win in z-Contact% and had a higher Hard Contact%. I know that a lot of people will point to the 4 year low in HR/FB and say he's not on the juice anymore after being caught but his hard contact rate was a career best at 41.5% last year, I have to believe the power is still there. The ballpark factors aren't greatly different between Safeco and Citi Field so I don't think the move will hamper Canó either. Steamer is conservative of course but has Canó behind by 3 runs, 4 HRs, 4 RBI and 4 SBs while winning average by more than 25 points. I'm not big on projections but being that close plus the fact that the shine of Canó has sunk him on about 25 picks after Shaw I think this choice is easy. This isn't quite a KO but it's an easy 10-7 on the cards in favor of Canó.

★ ★ ★ WINNER - ROBINSON CANÓ 10-9 ★ ★ ★

2019

IN THIS LEAGUE

Judges Scorecard

MATT MODICA	RYAN BLOOMFIELD	JAMES ANDERSON
CANÓ 10-9	SHAW 10-9	CANÓ 10-8

Round 62: Travis Shaw vs Robinson Canó

MATT OLSON VS IAN DESMOND

	MATT OLSON				IAN DESMOND	
AVG.	.247	★		AVG.		.236
HR	29	★	ROUND 63	HR		22
RBI	84			RBI	★	88
RUNS	85			RUNS	★	82
SB	2			SB	★	20

MATT OLSON

THE WELSH

Matt Olson had such a fantastic 2017 over a small amount of games, the expectations for him were sky high coming into 2018. I think there is a little disappointment since the average dipped, and he hit only five more home runs than the year before, but in 100 more games. What he's proved though, similar to the Travis Shaw conversation, is that we know what this guy is. We've got a 30-35 home run, 90/90+ runs and RBI first baseman. I'm a little bullish on the numbers, but even Steamer has him sitting at 32/81/90. Ian Desmond worries me a bit. I'm going on record, and say he doesn't repeat his 20/20 season. I think the stolen bases are more repeatable, but I'm not sure I am with it on the power. He had 18 first half home runs, and only four in the second. He had a wild split as well, with a first half 37.5% HR/FB, and only a 9.8% in the second half. These two are also on the opposite spectrum of contact, where Matt Olson had the 8th best hard hit percentage at 47.3%, and Ian Desmond had the ninth highest soft contact percentage at 21.5%. Desmond will clearly take the stolen bases, but Olson will firmly take HR/RBI/RUN. As much as I want to say Desmond has average, I'm not sure it's that far off between the two. The value isn't close to being a concern for me here, so it's Olson with a KO win.

IAN DESMOND

BOGMAN

I don't understand why Matt Olson is going 40 picks ahead of Ian Desmond even a little. The only thing I can think of is because Desmond is slated to hit 6th in the Rockies lineup, which makes no sense because that's where he put up those great numbers last season. It can't be that Desmond is going to regress by a ton because he literally had 0 career highs last season. Desmond did have somewhat of a power outage in the 2nd half but he was still stealing bases. Olson is a great power hitter and it wouldn't be surprising to see him go well over the 30 HR mark this season but it seems like drafters are trying to get the 2017 41.4% HR/FB and if we're buying that we might as well buy the 100 SB seasons that Billy Hamilton used to get in the minors. Olson did have a top 10 Hard Contact% which is very impressive but without the pure contact% to go with it the shine comes off a lot. Even with the potential to have a huge power season Olson still doesn't steal bases like Desmond does so at worst these two should be going right next to each other with Olson being the power upside guy and Desmond being the power/speed combo guy. Desmond is too good of a value to not win this one. I won't give it a KO but it would be a unanimous decision.

★ ★ ★ WINNER - MATT OLSON 10-8 ★ ★ ★

2019 | Judges Scorecard

KC BUBBA	JAKE CIELY	ROB SILVER
OLSON 10-7	OLSON 10-8	DESMOND 10-9

Round 63: Matt Olson vs Ian Desmond

MICHAEL BRANTLEY VS GREGORY POLANCO

	MICHAEL BRANTLEY				GREGORY POLANCO
AVG.	.309 ★			AVG.	.254
HR	17		★	HR	23
RBI	76 ★			RBI	81
RUNS	89 ★			RUNS	75
SB	12			SB	12

ROUND 64

MICHAEL BRANTLEY

THE WELSH

Michael Brantley's signing with the Astros might be one of the bigger impact signings that doesn't center around a 200 million dollar contract. Brantley is a perfect fit in Houston. Roster Resource has him hitting five, which would be a prime RBI spot behind Altuve and Correa. The reason why it's perfect, is that no one makes better contact than Brantley. He lead MLB in contact % at 90.9%, and contact percentage in the zone at 97.3%. He also had the lowest swinging strike percentage of anyone in baseball. Call me optimistic, but putting that kind of a contact hitter behind that young core of stars is a prime RBI opportunity waiting to happen. Steamer is pretty light on his numbers, but it's also light on the games, which is fair due to past injuries. This is another guy that I think is primed for a career year. I think Brantley could flirt with 2014 numbers, outside of the speed. I have little to no trust in Houston letting him run. 20/90/100/10 with a .290 average is very doable for a patient, contact based hitter in Houston, who should have guys on base left and right. Not to skip over Polanco so much, but the obvious is his injury, which should hold him back from starting the season. I like the power/speed combo, but average isn't an area of strength. Both of these guys are values. Brantley in the 120 draft range is a steal. Polanco is a fantastic post 200 stash who could beat expectations. Sadly though, this one isn't close with my call for career numbers from Brantley - one of the more dominating KO's yet. Brantley wins.

GREGORY POLANCO

BOGMAN

What an appropriate debate, the most injury prone OF in the last few years vs a player that will most likely start the season on the DL! I was all in on the Brantley train in 2018 and boy did he pay off! Brantley ended up playing in 143 games, led the league in Contact%, z-Contact% and was 5th in o-Contact% (balls swung on outside the strikezon), bottom line is the dude can hit when he's in there. He also ended up with the 2nd most Runs he's ever scored in a season, 2nd most HRs, 3rd most RBI, 3rd best batting average and hit double digit SBs. Brantley did all of that while starting off the season on the DL last year and Polanco finds himself in the same situation. I'm not sitting here telling you that Polanco is going to come off the DL in early April and then put career numbers but being a great performer especially when it counts down the stretch in H2H leagues isn't out of the realm of possibility. Obviously Polanco isn't a player you select when your team is flush with players who have spent extensive time on the DL but he's going after pick 200 and can be a great grab and stash player. The problem is we should probably only take one of these guys, I think Polanco has a teeny tiny bit more upside at his current value so I'd take him in a tough, most likely split decision.

★ ★ ★ WINNER - MICHAEL BRANTLEY 10-8 ★ ★ ★

2019 Judges Scorecard

IN THIS LEAGUE · FANTASY SPORTS · PODCAST NETWORK

CHRIS BLESSING	SAMMY REID	TIM HEANEY
BRANTLEY KO	POLANCO 10-9	BRANTLEY 10-9

Round 64: Michael Brantley vs Gregory Polanco

MALLEX SMITH VS BILLY HAMILTON

MALLEX SMITH			ROUND 65		BILLY HAMILTON	
AVG.	.296	★			AVG.	.236
HR	2			★	HR	4
RBI	40	★			RBI	29
RUNS	65			★	RUNS	74
SB	40	★			SB	34

MALLEX SMITH

BOGMAN

I'm not into drafting one trick ponies so I don't know that I'll actually own either of these guys this season but I'm done with trying to figure out Billy Hamilton. The old adage for speedsters says 'You can't steal first' and that has been Hamilton's issue for his entire career. Billy actually had a better contact rate than Mallex but his Hard Contact% was dead last among qualified hitters. Hamilton has never hit above .260 and while a career high of 59 SBs in a season is impressive he had 2 seasons of over 100 swipes in the minors and that has just never come to fruition in the bigs. The scenario for Hamilton doesn't look very good this season as he's going to relegated to hitting in the 9 hole for the Royals, they are willing to send a runner but that lineup probably won't turn over a lot. Mallex Smith is in a new situation in Seattle but his presence will force Dee Gordon to the bottom of the lineup while he hits leadoff. The Mariners were middle of the pack in SBs last season but will most likely send the runners a bit more as they've traded off a lot of their best hitters. Like I said before I'm probably not going to be taking either one of these guys but even with Hamilton going 75 or more picks after Smith I still see him as a wasted pick. If I have to take one it's Mallex by a nose, in boxing terms it's whoever lands more punches because neither one has the power to knock the other out.

BILLY HAMILTON

THE WELSH

Honestly, what are some positives we can say about Billy Hamilton right now? He's had a three year decline in average, on base, slugging, while only stealing 34 stolen bases. That stolen base total was the lowest since his debut where he played 13 games and stole 13 bases. I know it's not a good case when defending him, but can you pinpoint the positives? Mallex is coming off a full season, hitting .290, while raising his average almost 30 points, and finishing third in baseball with 40 stolen bases. Mallex is also set up for a full-time gig this season, and I see little reason he shouldn't hit at the top of the order. If I would pick on anything with Mallex, it's that you might want to temper batting average expectations a bit. He had the sixth highest BABIP of any player with 400 or more plate appearances. This doesn't mean he has to decline, but I'd be surprised to see .290 again. Let's say he gets on base less, but plays more games, it's going to be hard for him to not drop 40 stolen bases again. Back to Hamilton, is he worth defending? His decline is well known, but we keep coming back, because this is also the guy that stole 50+ bases four straight years. If you would take his lowest stolen base output over those four years, it would have beat the 2018 leader by 11. The past brings us back in. The hope on a new team is interesting. Hamilton should hit 9th though, where Mallex is hitting first, but I am very intrigued by how the Royals will use him in that lineup. It only matters if he gets on base, though. Here's one thing I can tell you - 11 players stole 30 or more bases last year; only two of those players have an ADP according to late January NFBC are going post 100. Billy Hamilton is the lowest by more than 40 spots to the next guy. Paying for the elite steals rebound has never been cheaper. Mallex might have the floor here, but you'll have to pay a near top 100 valuation on him. Hamilton is post 150. Hamilton has a rebound in the late rounds to win 10-9.

★ ★ ★ **WINNER - MALLEX SMITH 10-8** ★ ★ ★

20 19 | Judges Scorecard

PAUL SPORER	DEREK VAN RIPER	CHRIS MEANEY
SMITH 10-8	SMITH 10-8	HAMILTON 10-9

Round 65: Mallex Smith vs Billy Hamilton

JOSÉ QUINTANA VS CHARLIE MORTON

JOSÉ QUINTANA			CHARLIE MORTON	
WINS	13	★ WINS	15
ERA	4.03	★ ERA	3.13
WHIP	1.319	★ WHIP	1.162
K	158	★ K	201
IP	174.1 ★	IP	167.0

ROUND 66

JOSÉ QUINTANA

BOGMAN

Morton is the better pitcher here, he has the better record, ERA, WHIP, more Ks, fewer BBs, better SwStr%, better GB/FB ratio and better GB%. So we can go ahead and throw out the argument of who is the better pitcher, it's Morton. This one is all about cost, I have never been a Morton guy and even coming off of this great season in Houston I'm not going to buy in when he's going at this highest point ever right around pick 100. Charlie Morton has cracked 150 innings only 3 times in his career, 2018, 2014 and 2011. Charlie Morton has never cracked 200 innings. While José Quintana isn't sexy he is healthy, he hasn't missed a start in any of his 6 full seasons and his low over that time of 174 innings Morton has never hit. Quintana hasn't been great the past 2 seasons but the 3 seasons he pitched previous to that his high ERA was 3.36. What happens when Charlie Morton tweaks something and the Rays start using openers for him? I'm not gambling with that high of a pick on a guy that can barely pass 150 innings. I'll bank on Quintana returning to his 13'-16' 65-80 picks later over Morton staying healthy.

CHARLIE MORTON

THE WELSH

Openers, Curveballs and Spin Rate, Oh My! All the things that make up a Rays pitcher, right? Charlie Morton's signing with Tampa Bay made all the sense in the world coming off a fantastic season with Houston. Like Snell and Glasnow, he moves his pitches at a high rate, which has lead to his recent success. Morton looks to be one of the few trusted pitchers for the Rays to go deep into games. So, opener or not, Morton should be in for a full run with the Rays. Of the 21 pitchers who tallied 200 strikeouts, Morton had the third least innings pitched, behind just Chris Sale and James Paxton. Quintana used to be everyone's favorite "underrated" pitcher. Things went backwards with the Cubs, as 2018 he had his second straight four plus ERA, worst career B/9 and let the homers fly more than he had before. His second half walks dropped, but that was about it. Quintana's ADP has dropped below 180, which is intriguing from a bounce back perspective. His focus seems to have centered around higher strikeout numbers with the Cubs, so maybe his aggressiveness can pay off this year. But I'm not optimistic. Morton is easily my guy here. This is the difference between a draft target and a calculated late bet. I wouldn't be surprised if Quintana takes the wins department, but I'm counting on Morton for across the board stats. This is a Charlie Morton KO.

★ ★ ★ WINNER - CHARLIE MORTON 10-8 ★ ★ ★

2019

Judges Scorecard

JASON COLLETTE	NATE GRIMM	MATT MODICA
MORTON 10-8	MORTON 10-8	MORTON 10-9

Round 66: José Quintana vs Charlie Morton

BUSTER POSEY VS WILSON RAMOS

	BUSTER POSEY		ROUND		WILSON RAMOS	
AVG.	.284		67	★	AVG.	.306
HR	5			★	HR	15
RBI	41	★			RBI	70
RUNS	47	★			RUNS	39
SB	3	★			SB	0

BUSTER POSEY

THE WELSH

Posey isn't the same player that his name value still illicites. I hear Posey, and I think of the "must own" catcher. He's been on a counting stats decline over the last four years, mainly with home runs and RBI. 2018 was an major low, but it was due to a season long nagging hip injury. He was shut down toward the end of the year to have surgery to repair that hip. The hip all but zapped his ability to hit for power. Posey hasn't been an elite catcher for a while really, but he has been consistent as hell when on the field. Six straight years of 140 plus games from a catcher is unreal. Plus, since 2010 his lowest average season has been .284. In fact, his average was the second highest last year of all catchers with over 350 PA. Number one was Ramos who hit .306. Ramos moves to the Mets as one of the top fantasy catcher options for many people. He had some weird splits last year. He hit 14 of his 15 home runs in the first half, across 77 games. He then hit only one home run in the second half, which was only 33 games. He went from a 23 range HR/FB down to six. Woof. His average jumped above .330 for that second half when the power disappeared, so his value does adjust. I'm not a believer in the average, as his BABIP surged above .350 in 2018, when he's a career .300 guy. Posey might miss a little bit of time to start the season as he rehabs back from surgery, but I am in for his return this season. I've said it before, I am not into taking catchers high. I want values. Posey is going a round or two behind Ramos, so with the value, big jump in average and an offensive rebound I think we could get from Posey, this is a 10-8 win in Posey's favor.

WILSON RAMOS

BOGMAN

I'm not paying for Realmuto or Sánchez and I'm not stopping off here on the catcher train either! These two should both probably be sliding over to 1B because they are good hitters that aren't healthy. Ramos has never been healthy, he's been in the bigs for 8 full seasons and has played in 100 games only 3 times. Posey is going to be coming off of hip surgery to start the season so we'll see how he looks in spring training. The nice thing about these guys is that they both just rake. Ramos has hit over .300 in 2 of the last 3 seasons and he has a HR/FB ratio has been over 20% in all of those seasons which would be 4th at Catcher in that span. Posey is still hitting for average with .284 being his low over the last 3 seasons but his HR/FB has fallen 5 straight seasons and hit a career low of 4.7% last season. There are just so many other good players in the 140-150 range that I won't be taking either one of these guys but if I have to pick one give me power upside like I've always said so that would be Ramos. If this was a boxing match they would probably break each other's jaws in the 5th round and it would be a draw.

★ ★ ★ WINNER - WILSON RAMOS 10-8 ★ ★ ★

20 19

Judges Scorecard

JAKE CIELY	STEVE GARDNER	JAMES ANDERSON
POSEY 10-9	RAMOS 10-8	RAMOS 10-8

Round 67: Buster Posey vs Wilson Ramos

JESSE WINKER VS NOMAR MAZARA

	JESSE WINKER		ROUND		NOMAR MAZARA	
AVG.	.299 ★			AVG.	.258	
HR	7		**68**	★ HR	20	
RBI	43			★ RBI	77	
RUNS	38			★ RUNS	61	
SB	0			★ SB	1	

JESSE WINKER

BOGMAN

Unlike the catcher debate I LOVE where both of these guys are going. Mazara has hit 20 HRs on the nose 3 straight seasons but last year he did it in only 128 games. Mazara had a thumb injury that sapped his power and really bothered him for the entire 2nd half of the season but it did not require surgery after the season. Jesse Winker did require offseason surgery for a shoulder injury that he says has plagued him for years. Winker was able to begin a hitting program in the middle of January and should be good to go for spring training. Winker's issue now is that the Reds are heavy on OFs after acquiring Kemp and Puig in a trade. I just don't think that Schebler can realistically keep Winker off the field, Winker had a better contact% than Joey Votto last year and I have to believe that some power will come back with the shoulder being better. Winker's SwStr% was more than 10% better than Schebler's last year also, it's pretty clear who the better hitter is. I think these guys are both great deals with Mazara going around 150 and Winker going after 200 but give Winker the slight edge in value. I'll take them both so 10-9 scorecard victory for Jesse Winker!

NOMAR MAZARA

THE WELSH

Mazara has been on the brink of a breakout for what feels like two years now. Three straight seasons of 20 home runs, but he projects out in the 25 range on a full season. He was a monster in the first half, with a major cool off in the second. Mazara has some favorable projections when it comes to average, as every projection I've seen has him set for a career high on that front. Mazara's power is real as it could push 30 on a full season, with a low 150 range ADP. Winker was putting up a solid season before missing the final two months with the shoulder injury. The contact Winker makes actually reminds me of Michael Brantley without the stolen bases. He's an on-base monster having a higher walk percent than strikeout percentage, and hit the .400 OBP mark. There are no guarantees with the Reds new acquisitions, plus Nick Senzel is being given the chance to take the center field job. His power plays, like Brantley with a high average, and the hope of high runs or RBI. but coming off the injuries and the lack of assurances in the lineup leave some questions. Winker has the fun speculation feel, where Mazara is a power premium target post 125 in drafts for the outfield. Mazara with a 10-7 win.

★ ★ ★ WINNER - JESSE WINKER 10-9 ★ ★ ★

2019

Judges Scorecard

ALEX CHAMBERLAIN	CLAY LINK	RYAN BLOOMFIELD
MAZARA 10-9	DRAW	WINKER 10-8

Round 68: Jesse Winker vs Nomar Mazara

TYLER GLASNOW VS YUSEI KIKUCHI

*

	TYLER GLASNOW		ROUND 69		YUSEI KIKUCHI	
	WINS	2		★	WINS	14
	ERA	4.27		★	ERA	3.08
	WHIP	1.272		★	WHIP	1.033
	K	136		★	K	153
	IP	111.2		★	IP	163.2

*2018 NPB Stats

TYLER GLASNOW

BOGMAN

I don't know that Glasnow has gotten a fair shake yet but hopefully that is going to change this year. Glasnow doesn't even have 30 starts under his belt yet but the Rays don't have too many SP options for this year so this will be the make or break season for him in 2019. Glasnow's K/9 was up over 10 with TB, his BB/9 dropped down to about 3.1 (career 5.03) and his xFIP for the season was 3.47 over 2 runs down from 2017 and a run lower than 2016. The Rays gave Glasnow a little more control of his pitching game plan than he had in Pittsburgh and changed up his pitch mix a little bit and I think we are going to see great returns in 2019. Kikuchi is going to come off boards earlier as we get closer to the regular season because people are always willing to take a risk on the shiny new toy. The Mariners have already said that they're going to 'slightly limit' Kikuchi this year and they have already sold off a lot of assets even before the season starts. I have a little fear of the shutdown as well because the Mariners determined to do a quick rebuild so if they decide to set a hard innings limit on Kikuchi he could miss the fantasy playoffs for those of us in H2H leagues. Give me the upside of Glasnow in what should be his first season as a full time starter.

YUSEI KIKUCHI

THE WELSH

This debate is full of unknowns. Glasnow in Tampa has some positives, but the biggest negative potentially is the use of the opener. His strikeouts held nicely, but wins and quality starts will be hard to trust. He's already a bit walk happy, and hovers around a four ERA. Steamer projections give him more traditional starts, but ending around 135 innings for the year. His cost isn't too crazy, but I'm also not sure the positives outweigh the negatives by a ton. Kikuchi is the big unknown though. First he's coming over from Japan where a few years back he was a strikeout dominate pitcher. This previous year he suffered some injuries, his strikeouts dropped and he lost some control. He's expected to see pretty full workload as a starter. If we see more of the previous season's Kikuchi, the comp of a Maeda might be true. But we've also seen the recent success of a guy like Miles Mikolas, which gives hope. It's interesting he has a reasonable draft range, which we don't often see from the new shiny toys, especially post 150 in drafts. Uncertainty vs unknowns is the storyline. I more comfortable banking on the Kikuchi, even it was for the first few months where he could dominate US hitters who haven't seen him, and then trade him in your league. Kikuchi in a 10-8 win.

★ ★ ★ WINNER - YUSEI KIKUCHI 10-8 ★ ★ ★

20 19

IN THIS LEAGUE FANTASY SPORTS PODCAST NETWORK

Judges Scorecard

EDDY ALMAGUER	PAUL SPORER	NICK POLLACK
KIKUCHI 10-7	KIKUCHI 10-9	KIKUCHI 10-9

Round 69: Tyler Glasnow vs Yusei Kikuchi

RAFAEL DEVERS VS MIKE MOUSTAKAS

	RAFAEL DEVERS		ROUND		MIKE MOUSTAKAS	
AVG.	.240			★ AVG.	.251
HR	21		**70**	★ HR	28
RBI	66			★ RBI	95
RUNS	59			★ RUNS	66
SB	5 ★			SB	4

RAFAEL DEVERS

BOGMAN

This one is hard because I like both of these guys but I know that Devers will be hitting in one of the best lineups in baseball and as of now I have no idea where Moose is going to end up. Devers dealt with a myriad of nagging injuries last season including a knee injury early in the season, shoulder around the all star break, and then a hamstring strain in late July that he tried to come back early from and wound up costing him all but 6 games in August. Weird that among all of those injuries in the 2nd half that his ISO actually went up. BABIP is all I really have to explain the 40 point drop in average from his 58 game stint in 2017, it was .342 in 17 and dropped to .281 last year so he's probably closer to the .270ish hitter that Steamer projects him for. Moose is the better hitter, better in contact%, hard%, FB% but like I've said many times throughout this book the bottom line in fantasy is the 5 categories that we acquire stats in. Devers is going to be driving in the top of that Red Sox lineup so even if he isn't as great a pure hitter as Moose he will most likely have more opportunities to drive in runs and be driven in. If Moose signs in the middle of a great lineup I'll change my tune but give me the youngster with upside and lineup talent in a narrow scorecard win.

MIKE MOUSTAKAS

THE WELSH

Why do people not like Moustakas? I just don't get it. He's not an elite 3B option, but he's the perfect, "when the dust settles" at 3B option. If I can't get my guy early, I'll probably take Moustakes every time post 100. As of writing this, he hasn't signed, and that could play a bit into potential boosts in production. Over the last two years though, he's averaged 33 home runs, 70 runs, 90 RBI and a .260 average. I've loved Devers since day one, but he's been inconsistent, and I wonder how patient the Red Sox will be. Devers had three months in 2018 that he hit under .215. The positive was his HR/FB raised into the twenties in the second half, as well he dropped his K% and upped his walk% both by a few percent. I think there was some sophomore adjustments in play. Long term I believe Devers is a .280 range hitter, who pushes 30 home runs, I'm just not so sure it's this year. He'll also be hitting lower in the lineup, which is less than desirable. These two are going right next two each other, and the only reason I can think is the unnamed home for Moustakas. If you're reading this and he has a home that doesn't completely deplete power like Seattle, this is a no brainer for 2019 in Moustakas' favor. A 10-7 win for Moose, and maybe finally a multi-year contract.

★ ★ ★ WINNER - RAFAEL DEVERS 10-9 ★ ★ ★

2019 Judges Scorecard

JOE PISAPIA	SAMMY REID	KC BUBBA
DEVERS 10-8	**DEVERS 10-9**	**MOUSTAKAS 10-9**

Round 70: Rafael Devers vs Mike Moustakas

KYLE SCHWARBER VS MIGUEL SANÓ

			ROUND 71			
AVG.	.238	★		AVG.	.199	
HR	26	★		HR	13	
RBI	61	★		RBI	41	
RUNS	64	★		RUNS	32	
SB	4	★		SB	0	

KYLE SCHWARBER

THE WELSH

It's eerie how close these two show up on Steamer. I mean they are projected as almost the same player. Sanó was a sinking ship with his average last year. He was at least 40 points under his career BABIP, which creates some optimism he can turn that around. He's a 20+ HR/ FB career guy, so if he makes better contact with a little luck he should pop around 30 home runs. Schwarber I think created his reality. There now is a reasonable expectation on his numbers in the .240 30 home run range. No longer catcher eligible, and just a left fielder drags his value a bit. This also gives the edge to Sanó due to position. Both guys holding similar skill sets, leaves us in a holding pattern. One major worry I have with Sanó was the strikeout numbers. Schwarber is no Joey Votto here with a 27.5% K percentage, but Sanó had a 38.5% K percentage and a 15.2% swinging strike percentage. That swing rate puts him in the Gallo and Davis territory without the big returns. Both guys hover in the top 200 ADP range. Even though position is a benefit to Sanó, I don't trust him rebounding. Schwarber should be hitting around the five spot in prime RBI territory, and a bit more trustworthy. I can't see myself owning either of these guys unless it was an OBP league, where there is a big boost for Schwarber. The match goes 10-8 to Schwarber.

MIGUEL SANÓ

BOGMAN

Holy shit is the shine off of these guys... Sanó has had any kind of problem you can imagine, hitting problems, fielding problems, legal problems and weight problems. Schwarber hasn't been the disaster that Sano is but the only plus tool he seems to have power, he couldn't stick at catcher, he blew out his knee in the OF in 2016, he's had a bit of weight issues but not as bad as Sanó and his defense isn't a disaster anymore but he's still going to get pulled for Almora in the late innings. Needless to say they both have something to prove this season but Sano especially does. Before last season Sano seemed kind of like a guy that was figuring it out especially in 2017 when he raised his average 28 points from 16 and he had an incredible HR/FB rate of 27.5%. I don't expect that to come all the way back but I think with a full season he could hit .250 with 30 bombs. I don't think that's out of the realm of possibility for Schwarber either but Sanó is the cheaper of the two so if I have to go with one I'll take Sanó. This is the last chance for Sanó if he doesn't come through here I can't imagine him being draftable next year. Get up of the mat and finish it Sanó!

★ ★ ★ WINNER - KYLE SCHWARBER 10-9 ★ ★ ★

2019 | Judges Scorecard

MATT MODICA	DEREK VAN RIPER	NATE GRIMM
DRAW	SCHWARBER 10-8	SCHWARBER 10-9

Round 71: Kyle Schwarber vs Miguel Sanó

PETER ALONSO VS ERIC HOSMER

PETER ALONSO			ROUND 72		ERIC HOSMER	
AVG.	.285 ★			AVG.	.253	
HR	36 ★			HR	18	
RBI	119 ★			RBI	69	
RUNS	92 ★			RUNS	72	
SB	0			★ SB	7	

*2018 MiLB Stats

PETER ALONSO
BOGMAN

I'm not usually one for taking the hitter that we know won't be in the bigs until later in the season but Alonso has HUGE power and there isn't much holding him back with the Mets. Alonso hit 36 HRs between AA and AAA last season and Steamer already has him projected to hit one more HR than Hosmer in 38 fewer games. The bat speed is unreal, The Welsh and I watched him turn on a 104 MPH fastball and put it over the wall in the AFL a few months back. I don't expect the average for Alonso to blow anyone away as he's not really a contact hitter. Last season Alonso's K% was 18.3% in AA but jumped to 25.9% when he got to AAA, he also dropped from a 52.6% FB rate in AA to 44.2% in AAA. Even if he winds up putting the ball on the ground more it'll be tough for him to match Hosmer's career high 60.4% GB rate from last season. What's even worse is that Hosmer could only muster a 19.7% FB rate which was second worst among qualified batters last season. Obviously you have to be fairly confident or have deep benches to be able to stash Alonso but I don't want ANY part of Eric Hosmer so I'd rather take a stash with HUGE upside. Easy early round KO for Alonso.

ERIC HOSMER
THE WELSH

I wish there was something easy to pinpoint Hosmer's issues in San Diego, besides him just not being that good. His Average took a huge nosedive. He had a five to six percent drop across the board on his contact numbers. Both from in and out of the zone. He also marked a career high in swinging strike percentage, which led to a career high in strikeouts. He is a below average first baseman who lost the redeeming factors that kept him drafted when he was missing big power numbers. Alonso on the other hand is all power. His 60 odd games in Triple-A, put up a better season than Hosmer across the majors. Alonso spent time in the Arizona Fall League where I spent a lot of time scouting him. His average dipped there, but his power shined, highlighted by hitting a 104 MPH Nate Pearson fastball out during the Fall Stars game. There are long term questions on his average, but I am not going to let than stop me. Steamer backs up a theory of mine that 120 games of Alonso will be more valuable than Hosmer. They put 90 games on his projection, and have him hitting 18 home runs. Hosmer is sitting on 21 home runs in 148 projected games. There are some potential blocks in New York, but Alonso is going to get significant time. They only thing I think holds him back is an extended hitless streak. Alonso is going in the 250 range where Hosmer is in the 160's. This is a hard pass for Hosmer, and a flier pick on Alonso is easy. Alonso with the KO.

★ ★ ★ WINNER - ERIC HOSMER 10-9 ★ ★ ★

2019 Judges Scorecard

IN THIS LEAGUE · FANTASY SPORTS · PODCAST NETWORK

ROB SILVER	JAMES ANDERSON	CHRIS BLESSING
HOSMER 10-9	DRAW	HOSMER 10-8

Round 72: Peter Alonso vs Eric Hosmer

JON GRAY VS KYLE HENDRICKS

	JON GRAY			KYLE HENDRICKS
WINS	12		★ WINS	14
ERA	5.12	ROUND	★ ERA	3.44
WHIP	1.346	**73**	★ WHIP	1.146
K	183 ★		K	161
IP	172.1		★ IP	199.0

JON GRAY

THE WELSH

Colorado pitchers amirte! It's really tough to get behind them. This being said, when Márquez and Freeland made huge strides and are targets for a lot of people this year. Gray was the guy everyone wanted last year. His strikeout numbers are a big portion of what is pulling us in. He had a 9.56 K/9, which is right in line with where we'd like it to be. He also had a sub three BB/9, which is something I'm always looking for. His home runs were out of control last year, and it's hard to project a Colorado pitcher with home run issues to make a massive change. Gray though, did have one of the biggest ERA to xFIP differentials. His 5.12 ERA sucked, but he had a 3.47 xFIP. That leaves some major questions of him possibly being able to get a hold of his ERA in the future. Hendricks is a very league average pitcher. Possibly just above average for fantasy. He rocks a three ERA, wich a sub two walk rate, but he's far from a strikeout guy. Hendricks is going before guys like Carlos Martínez and Masahiro Tanaka in NFBC, which I don't get at all. I'd rather speculate on strikeouts, and the fixed ERA with Gray in the 190 range. If Gray does push his ERA to say 3.6 or 3.7, he'll jump Hendricks quite a bit due to those strikeouts. Gray with a 10-9 win.

KYLE HENDRICKS

BOGMAN

These guys can not get more opposite. Kyle Hendricks is the stable easy going starting pitcher that isn't sexy but you know exactly what you're getting. How many times has Hendricks had 4.00+ ERA? Never. He's been over 3.50 only once and that was in 2015! Hendricks isn't going to blow you away with Ks but he'll dazzle you with his WHIP NEVER going over 1.20 in his career. He's the kind of man every woman wants, easy going, stable, 401K, great father, nice to your friends. Jon Gray has the sexy strikeout ability although his K/9 has never gone over 10. Gray isn't prone to the blow up or anything but he gave up 5 or more runs in 11 of his 31 starts but he never gave up more than 7 and that was only once. His ERA was actually better the 3rd time through the order than it was the 2nd time (5.31 to 6.02) neither were good but that is uncommon. Gray has never had an ERA under 3.50 and he's never had a WHIP under 1.30. The only redeeming factor for Jon Gray is his xFIP was 1.65 runs lower than his actual ERA so there could be a decent return but I'll let someone else find out. Give me the stable breadwinner Kyle Hendricks in a gentleman's fight and shake hands when it's over!

★ ★ ★ WINNER - KYLE HENDRICKS 10-8 ★ ★ ★

20 19

Judges Scorecard

ENO SARRIS	RYAN BLOOMFIELD	STEVE GARDNER
HENDRICKS 10-8	HENDRICKS 10-9	HENDRICKS 10-7

Round 73: Jon Gray vs Kyle Hendricks

BRANDON NIMMO VS HARRISON BADER

BRANDON NIMMO

AVG.	.263
HR	17 ★
RBI	47 ★
RUNS	77 ★
SB	9

ROUND 74

HARRISON BADER

★ AVG.	.264
HR	12
RBI	37
RUNS	61
★ SB	15

BRANDON NIMMO

BOGMAN

This one looks close but I'm not sure that it actually is. These dudes both got their first crack at full time starting jobs in the bigs and came through for their teams. Nimmo was the leadoff hitter for most of his games and he'll stick there this season, Bader hit 7th in the lineup and it doesn't look like he'll have a chance to move up without an injury. Nimmo won't steal many bases, the 9-10 range is probably about right for him but he's a leadoff hitter because of his crazy high OBP boosted by his 15% BB rate which he's kept over the last two seasons. A finger injury seemed to take a bit of the power out of the bat in the 2nd half for Nimmo as he hit 14 of his 17 in the first half so we might be able to expect a little more in the power department but I wouldn't put money on it. The drop to 8 in the lineup and the fact that the Cardinals refuse to move José Martínez has me a bit concerned for Bader. The high K% (29.3%) and low BB% (7.3%) will probably keep him low in the lineup. Bader didn't hit poorly against righties at .251 but Martínez killed them at .313 so I'm a bit worried about rest days although Fowler is a tweak away from making them both everyday players. Nimmo is just a better hitter in a better spot in the lineup so I'm going to say this an easy 10-8ish victory for him.

HARRISON BADER

THE WELSH

This is another one of those debates where I'm like, geez who thought of this, this is hard. Oh yeah, we did. They mirror each other in a lot of ways. More runs than RBI, sub 20 power, high strikeout, but valuable in the range they are going off at. Nimmo looks to have the leadoff spot on early depth charts, which I think is an added plus. Bader looks to be hitting eight, which is less than ideal. One worry I have defending my guy here, is the potential platoon situation that we could have with Tyler O'Neill. Bader for fantasy holds the cards here with the stolen bases. If power, average, runs and RBI are relative, with small swings in either direction, Bader's chance at 15-20 stolen bases give him a clear advantage. Steamer agrees by giving Bader the advantage in every category but runs, and in less games. Both teams boosted their offenses, but St. Louis takes that advantage with the addition of Goldy. These two are going literally next to each other, so there is no value. This may be as close as it's laid out, but when in doubt, give the advantage to the guy who steals the bases. 10-9 win for Bader.

★ ★ ★ WINNER - BRANDON NIMMO 10-9 ★ ★ ★

2019 Judges Scorecard

JAKE CIELY	JASON COLLETTE	SAMMY REID
NIMMO 10-9	NIMMO 10-9	NIMMO 10-8

Round 74: Brandon Nimmo vs Harrison Bader

YOÁN MONCADA

VS

GARRETT HAMPSON
*

	YOÁN MONCADA				GARRETT HAMPSON	
AVG.	.235			★	AVG.	.311
HR	17 ★		ROUND		HR	10
RBI	61 ★		**75**		RBI	40
RUNS	73			★	RUNS	81
SB	12			★	SB	36

2018 MiLB Stats

YOÁN MONCADA

BOGMAN

Well we have more opposites here. We are looking at SB upside for Hampson here as he stole 38 between 3 levels last season and 51 at high A in 2017. He's a college bat that has hit .300 in every stop he's made in the minors so there's no need to think he won't hit .300 or close to it in a full season in the bigs. Hampson doesn't have much power upside which is unfortunate because he's in that great Rockies lineup but Coors will probably get him up to 10ish range. Moncada had the speed upside as well stealing 49 in his first taste single A, 45 between high A and AA the following season, down to 20 between AAA and the bigs in 17 and all the way down to 12 in his first full season of starting. Moncada does have power upside though as he hit 17 last season. Boiling this down here Hampson will probably win average and SB while Moncada gets Runs as the White Sox #2 hitter, HRs as he actually has power and RBI. Should Hampson struggle the Rockies have all kinds of options as well with Brendan Rodgers possibly shifting to second or if Murphy is feeling spry he could slide back from 1B to 2B and Desmond can play 1st, the White Sox will have Moncada playing come hell or high water. The average drop for Moncada doesn't scare me as much as Hampson getting platooned or sent back down, give me Yoan Moncada Now!

GARRETT HAMPSON

THE WELSH

Hampson has everyone hot and bothered. In 2018 during his two levels of the minors, he hit 10 homers, stole 36 bases and hit above .300 at both levels. He's essentially been handed the second base job, as recently signed Daniel Murphy looks to be playing first base. Moncada was a big disappointment last season, falling short of most expectations, with his average being the one that went heavily in the wrong direction. I want to be a believer in Moncada this year, and to be honest, I will speculate on some shares, but this is a very make or break year in my eyes for him. He topped 200 strikeouts. His second half wasn't great, as he saw his HR/FB drop under 10, and his hard hit percentage dropped by five percent. We dream on his five tools, which has now probably turned to four, with his average being a dream more than a reality. The problem with the gamble is what it may do to your roster construction. That low average can kill you, whereas Hampson is sitting in .290 range even on most projections. I'm a little sour on the 30+ stole base thing, where I see Hampson a little more like early D.J. LeMahieu with the average and runs, but solid stolen bases. Hampson's floor is much higher here, but my personal bias can only give this a 10-9 edge over Moncada.

★ ★ ★ WINNER - GARRETT HAMPSON 10-8 ★ ★ ★

20 19

Judges Scorecard

IN THIS LEAGUE | FANTASY SPORTS PODCAST NETWORK

JOE PISAPIA	EDDY ALMAGUER	ITL ARMY
HAMPSON 10-7	MONCADA 10-8	HAMPSON 10-7 (77%)

Round 75: Yoán Moncada vs Garrett Hampson

SALVADOR PEREZ VS WILLSON CONTRERAS

	SALVADOR PEREZ		ROUND 76		WILLSON CONTRERAS
AVG.	.235			★ AVG.	.249
HR	27 ★			HR	10
RBI	80 ★			RBI	54
RUNS	52 ★			RUNS	50
SB	1			★ SB	4

SALVADOR PÉREZ

THE WELSH

Last year I made a big case for passing on Gary Sánchez and his high price tag, to get similar production over 100 picks later with Salvador Pérez. Salvador lead all catchers last season in home runs and RBI. He did all of that, even with his average dipping to its lowest career total. A positive side on that front, was his BABIP followed his average, dropping around 40 points lower than his career totals. Contreras bounced off his career year by cutting his home runs in half over 21 more games, and dropping his average almost 30 points. We've preached here how much we aren't paying high prices or jumping ahead to make sure we secure a catcher. That doesn't change here. I personally would love to have Salvy, as there aren't many that are as consistent and trustworthy in three departments at the positions than him. What I don't like, is his cost rising near the top 100 in drafts. But even though Contreras is now falling into the 130 range, it wouldn't make me shy from grabbing Pérez regardless of the savings. This is a 10-7 Salvador Pérez win!

WILLSON CONTRERAS

BOGMAN

More catchers in the first half of the draft! No thank you, although on occasion I've seen these guys sink much farther than that in one catcher only leagues. Contreras let us down so much in the 2018 that he (and Gary Sánchez) are big reasons that I am just done with catchers. It's really hard to pinpoint the reason of Contreras' fall off from 17-18. He did start to see more breaking balls and his Hard Contact% dropped way off and his soft contact% raised a lot so that basically is what we have to go with. It really seems like pitchers just gave him less to hit but he actually saw a higher percentage of strikes by more than 1% in 2018. Contreras did see more more balls being thrown low and outside so the league basically adjusted on him and he didn't adjust back. Another reason I've heard kicked around is that he was concerned with the goings on in his home country of Venezuela. Salvador Pérez is easy to figure out, he's hit 20 HRs in 4 straight seasons including 27 on the nose two years in a row, he's been between 64-80 RBI, his average has took a dip last season but that can be explained away by an early season knee injury so it'll be in the .250ish range. So it's basically a gamble on Contreras returning to form or taking the standard Salvador Pérez line and if I'm taking a catcher in the 130-140ish range I might as well gamble on upside. Contreras in a close one.

★ ★ ★ WINNER - SALVADOR PÉREZ 10-8 ★ ★ ★

20 19 — IN THIS LEAGUE — *Judges Scorecard*

ALEX CHAMBERLAIN	ROB SILVER	TIM HEANEY
PÉREZ 10-8	PÉREZ 10-9	PÉREZ 10-8

Round 76: Salvador Pérez vs Willson Contreras

FELIPE VÁZQUEZ VS RAISEL IGLESIAS

	FELIPE VÁZQUEZ			ROUND			RAISEL IGLESIAS	
SAVES	37	★				SAVES	30	
ERA	2.70			**77**		★ ERA	2.38	
WHIP	1.243					★ WHIP	1.069	
K	89	★				K	80	
IP	70.0					★ IP	72.0	

FELIPE VÁZQUEZ

THE WELSH

These are your prime, "post top closer" targets. Vázquez is firmly going over Iglesias, but to be honest here, Rasiel is a 100% target of mine for 2019. Projections only have Iglesias sitting around three and a half on his ERA, but Rasiel has had a two and a half ERA for three straight years. His FIP has sat in the threes, but he is a known FIP beater. Follow me here, Iglesias is the Khris Davis of closers. Three straight years with that ERA, 70 innings pitched, 10+ K/9 and averaging 29 saves over the last two years (he wasn't really closing in 2016). Now I know I'm writing for Vázquez, but I want you to know where I am at on Iglesias. Vázquez was sixth in all of baseball with those 37 saves. Besides the tick up in strikeouts, he mirrored Kimbrel in many ways last year. I don't love the top 90 price on Vázquez, which makes me lean more Iglesias, but the consistency Vázquez has shown, as well as strikeout numbers can't be denied. This is a super close 10-9 win for Vázquez that could go either way.

RAISEL IGLESIAS

BOGMAN

I have to be honest here, I don't think that Iglesias is a better pitcher than Vázquez. I do think the difference is so small that I'll take whoever costs less and that is clearly Iglesias right now. Vázquez is the winner in ERA, xFIP, the BABIP was 100 points higher on his end, he had a way more realistic LOB% at 77.7% to 91.6% (which was the 2nd highest among pitchers with 70 IP or more), better GB/FB rate, more Ks, fewer BBs, more saves, allowed less hard contact, you get the idea. Iglesias had some stats go his way as well, WHIP, overall contact%, soft contact% and SwStr%. All of these outside of LOB% were close enough to basically call it a wash so this really comes down to cost and which team you think will get more save opportunities. Pittsburgh won 15 more games than Cincinnati last season but I have to think with the improvements made to the lineup and the Reds being in the market to acquire a big time starter these teams will be much closer in 2019. Iglesias is going 15-20 spots lower in the draft right now so with everything else being fairly close I'll go with Iglesias at a lower cost.

★ ★ ★ WINNER - FELIPE VÁZQUEZ KO ★ ★ ★

2019 | Judges Scorecard

PAUL SPORER	KC BUBBA	CHRIS MEANEY
VÁZQUEZ KO	VÁZQUEZ 10-8	VÁZQUEZ KO

Round 77: Felipe Vázquez vs Raisel Iglesias

J.A. HAPP VS RICH HILL

			ROUND 78			
WINS	17 ★				WINS	11
ERA	3.65 ★				ERA	3.66
WHIP	1.131			★	WHIP	1.123
K	193 ★				K	150
IP	177.2 ★				IP	132.2

J.A. HAPP

BOGMAN

I think it's safe to say that J.A. Happ felt comfortable in Pinstripes last year. Happ went 7-0 in 11 starts after being traded the Yankees last season and his ERA with the Yankees 2.69 after being 4.18 with the Jays. 7 of those 11 starts for the Yankees were at home where he had a 2.72 ERA it looks like we don't need to fear the #1 ballpark factor for HRs over the last 3 seasons in Yankee stadium. Happ's GB/FB rate wasn't exactly stellar at 0.95, neither was his GB/FB% at 13.4%, but Hill was right there with him (0.97 and 14.7%) pitching his home games in one of the better ballpark factor stadiums for pitchers in Dodger Stadium. I'll never own Rich Hill, regardless of cost, because of his inability to stay healthy. Hill has had his 'healthiest' 3 season stretch of his career and he hasn't gone over 135.2 innings in those seasons. The Dodgers have actually done a good job of resting him but he's one of the most injury prone players in MLB history and he turns 39 before the season starts. J.A. has thrown 145+ innings in 5 straight seasons and he's averaged 15+ wins the last 3 of those seasons. Now Happ is playing with a team that will give him an incredible amount of run support. This debate is easy take Happ between these two even with the 60ish pick difference.

RICH HILL

THE WELSH

Rich Hill is so brutal every year. He's that guy, where if he could just put in a 200 innings, we'd be talking about a top 20 to 25 pitcher. He has never done that once in his career though. Here's what you can count on, somewhere from 120-150 innings,10+ K/9 per nine and a sub three BB/9. What you cannot count on is health and upside. That upside is all about innings, and the guy cannot stay on the field, which sucks. I lovingly refer to him as "Blister God." Happ was traded to the Yankees, where he saw solid success in his 11 starts with a 7-0 record and a 2.69 ERA. His FIP sat in the 4 range, which is something to monitor. Due to that success and maybe a little of that Yankee boost, Happ is sitting in the top 140 range. Hill on the other end is going post 160, which is probably relative for his volatility. I'm not super excited about either of these guys, but with Hill you just don't find that kind of elite strikeout rate and a controlled ERA that late in drafts. Maybe if you hit it big on a prospect who gets huge season run (makes me think of the year José Fernández was called up in March by the Marlins), but that is few and far between. Hill with a 10-8 win.

★ ★ ★ WINNER - J.A. HAPP 10-9 ★ ★ ★

2019

IN THIS LEAGUE *Judges Scorecard*

DEREK VAN RIPER	NICK POLLACK	MATT MODICA
HAPP 10-9	HAPP 10-8	HAPP 10-9

Round 78: J.A. Happ vs Rich Hill

BYRON BUXTON VS ENDER INCIARTE

	BYRON BUXTON		ROUND 79		ENDER INCIARTE

	BUXTON				INCIARTE
AVG.	.156			★ AVG.	.265
HR	0			★ HR	10
RBI	4			★ RBI	61
RUNS	8			★ RUNS	83
SB	5			★ SB	28

BYRON BUXTON

THE WELSH

This one kind of feels a little like the Hampson vs Moncada debate. This is a very floor vs ceiling debate. Inciarte was a pleasant stolen base surprise, but otherwise an average option. Buxton has all the tools, but hasn't gotten them to work. Buxton's 28 games were an absolute disaster, and the Twins just sent him down to get things together. The results were also so so. The fact that he's still a low single digit walk percentage, and an almost 30 percent strikeout rate is more than concerning. The positives, well he did add around 20 pounds of muscle in the off-season, renewed focus and a clean slate. I'm a sucker for tooled out discounts, and that's what he is. Steamer gives the home run edge to Buxton, but Inciarte takes the other four categories. If we didn't have that 2017 season, where he hit 17 home runs, stole 20 bases and hit .253, I think it would be easier to quit the former top prospect. The fact that he's only 25, and from an at-bat perspective, this would really be like his third full season, I have to go Buxton. Inciarte is safe, but enjoy the 50 spot discount and scratch that lottery ticket.

ENDER INCIARTE

BOGMAN

When I say we need to 'fear the bottom-out' I can't think of a better example than 2018 Byron Buxton. The underlying numbers have never been favorable for Buxton, he's never had a great contact% (70.1% career), his K% last year was high (29.4%) and his BABIP was high at .339. We have seen players succeed with way worse outliers though so to see the total and complete collapse was unexpected. Buxton only saw 94 PA but his contact% was actually up, the hard contact% was up and the soft contact% was lower. Buxton's BABIP was 113 points lower last season even with the the better contact and hitting the ball harder, he actually hit's better against the shift too so that wasn't it either. Injuries could explain it, Buxton was plagued by thumb, wrist and toe ailments all season. In any case, Inciarte is the anti-Buxton, he had the 11th highest Contact% among qualified hitters, he doesn't have much power but he's gotten to 10 HRs 2 straight seasons and his SBs have increased 3 seasons in a row. The SBs did fall off in the 2nd half in 18, when Acuña came up they had him hit leadoff but for 2019 Inciarte is going to move back to one and Acuña will slide down to cleanup. Inciarte had a career high 23 SBs in just the first half last year hitting leadoff and he'll have Donaldson and Acuña driving him in this year. I'm not against taking a flier on Buxton but Inciarte ain't a flier. Early round KO.

★ ★ ★ WINNER - ENDER INCIARTE 10-9 ★ ★ ★

20 19

Judges Scorecard

STEVE GARDNER	JASON COLLETTE	NATE GRIMM
BUXTON 10-9	INCIARTE 10-9	INCIARTE 10-8

Round 79: Byron Buxton vs Ender Inciarte

ROBERTO OSUNA VS SEAN DOOLITTLE

	ROBERTO OSUNA		ROUND 80		SEAN DOOLITTLE
SAVES	21			★ SAVES	25
ERA	2.37			★ ERA	1.60
WHIP	0.974			★ WHIP	0.600
K	32			★ K	60
IP	38.0			★ IP	45.0

ROBERTO OSUNA — THE WELSH

I'm not sure there is one player who is more excited for a new start than Osuna. Filled with legal trouble throughout 2018, followed by a trade that had a bunch of public backlash, Osuna looks for a reboot to 2019. Once traded to Houston, Osuna had 1.99 ERA, a sub one WHIP and 12 saves in 23 games he pitched in. Doolittle was great in the 45 innings that he pitched last year, but fun fact, Doolittle hasn't reached 52 innings pitched in a season since 2014. Where Osuna has off the field issues that seem to be over, Doolittle has on the field ones. Projections are pretty weary of Doolittle this year, as Steamer only has him getting 22 saves. Osuna on the other hand now closes for one of the best teams in baseball, and should be flooded with save opportunities. They are also going to welcome some stability at the closer position. Doolittle makes this close since I don't want to pay premium prices on closers, but Osuna is the better option. He's also in another tier, that makes this an easy pick with a 10-7 win.

SEAN DOOLITTLE — BOGMAN

Good thing this isn't a popularity contest right? While Roberto Osuna is a dirtbag, he can close games and Houston is a good place to do it. He got his 2nd chance and he's being drafted inside the top 100 because of his situation. I know that Houston is a better team than Washington but the difference in saves last year was only 6 in the Astros favor and that was with 23 more wins than the Nationals. In the NL East the Braves won the division in 2018, the Nationals have added Corbin to the staff, the Phillies are throwing around money to bring in FAs and the Mets have made significant improvements to their lineup. We could see a nice little influx of tight games for the Nationals this year. The AL East has seen the Rangers do little to improve, the Mariners sell off, the Angels will be without Ohtani pitching the entire season and is the A's 97 win 2018 repeatable? The only team that had more 4+ run victories than the Astros last season was the World Champion Red Sox. If that doesn't convince you Doolittle was better in W, SV, ERA, WHIP, K/9, xFIP, BABIP, LOB%, SwStr% and had a lower Hard Contact%. Doolittle also goes off the board about 20 picks later. Doolittle wins a fair fight with a member of the same gender.

★ ★ ★ WINNER - ROBERTO OSUNA 10-9 ★ ★ ★

20 19 | Judges Scorecard

ALEX CHAMBERLAIN	RYAN BLOOMFIELD	JAKE CIELY
OSUNA 10-8	DOOLITTLE 10-9	OSUNA 10-9

Round 80: Roberto Osuna vs Sean Doolittle

JON LESTER VS DALLAS KEUCHEL

	JON LESTER			ROUND		DALLAS KEUCHEL	
WINS	18	★		**81**		WINS	12
ERA	3.32	★				ERA	3.74
WHIP	1.310	★				WHIP	1.314
K	149				★	K	153
IP	181.2				★	IP	204.2

JON LESTER

BOGMAN

I understand that Jon Lester is getting older but what does that really mean for him? Maybe he'll end up on the DL this year? He's had 31 or more starts in 11 straight years. Sure maybe a little shine comes off the apple the last few years, his K/9, BB/9 and GB/FB rate have dropped 4 years in a row. He did seem to have a hiccup in 17 where that ERA climbed over 4 but he got in back to under 3.50 last year where it's been 4 of the last 5 seasons. Dallas Keuchel does keep the ball on the ground with the highest GB% in the bigs last season but he had the highest fielding% in the bigs behind him last year. As I'm writing this I'm not sure where he's going to end up but Cincinnati was the rumor and they were middle of the pack in fielding% which meant about 30 more errors than the Astros. Couple more errors for Keuchel wouldn't be great as the ERA climbs up over 5 on his 3rd time through the order. Philly is spending some money, they almost doubled the amount of errors the Astros had. Houston also ranked below league average in ballpark factors for runs and HRs over the last 3 seasons. Honestly I like other pitchers in the neighborhood of where Lester and Keuchel are going but if I get sniped and I'm stuck picking between these guys give old man river, I know what I'm getting.

DALLAS KEUCHEL

THE WELSH

At this stage, I don't think either of these guys are going to be the type of pitchers who give you back massive returns or carry your fantasy teams. But both are the type of consistent options that bolster up your rotation. I like Keuchel a few notches better even without a current destination as of writing this. Putting Keuchel in Cincinnati would create a few more questions and concerns than many other locations, so keep this in mind. 2018 Keuchel was far from spectacular, but consistent across the entire season. Lester fell off in the second half adding two runs more per game to his ERA. Lester to his credit though, in unspectacular fashion has had 15 or more wins in four of the last six seasons. Keuchel in his consistency has kept his ERA and xFIP incredibly close, where Lester posted a 4.43 xFIP. That xFIP spilled into his projections where he is lined for a 4.35 ERA to most projections. Even though the strikeouts tick a tad more to Lester and we know his home, I lean Keuchel. We're not too far removed from his Cy Young season, and though he isn't the same guy, I think there is a bit more in the tank,. If you want to play safe, Lester makes sense. I score this 10-9 in favor of Keuchel.

★ ★ ★ **WINNER - DALLAS KEUCHEL 10-9** ★ ★ ★

20 19 | *Judges Scorecard*

ENO SARRIS	SAMMY REID	TIM HEANEY
KEUCHEL 10-8	**KEUCHEL 10-7**	**DRAW**

Round 81: Jon Lester vs Dallas Keuchel

RYAN BRAUN vs AUSTIN MEADOWS

	RYAN BRAUN			AUSTIN MEADOWS
AVG.	.254		AVG. ★	.287
HR	20 ★	ROUND	HR	6
RBI	64 ★	**82**	RBI	17
RUNS	59 ★		RUNS	19
SB	11 ★		SB	5

RYAN BRAUN   BOGMAN

God. Damn. It. I don't know how I got stuck with the lying cheater for this debate but begrudgingly I actually believe in drafting Braun over Meadows because of the stupid draft value. I need to reevaluate my life. Anyway, yes Braun is 35 and hasn't played in 150+ games since 2012 but he also has played in at least 125 in 4 of the last 5 seasons. I'm not so worried about games played between Braun and Meadows because Meadows has missed a lot of minor league time with injuries. Couple the minor league injury issues with the fact that this will be his first full season with a big league team and the Rays have another big prospect Jesus Sanchez in the OF I think playing time could end up being a wash. Meadows makes more contact overall (82.7%-79.6%) but Braun makes more hard (43%-37.1%) and less soft contact (16.4%-20%), leading me to believe that Meadows will hit for a better average and Braun will have more power. The real fear in this debate is missing out on a huge year from a new player with good upside and the cliff drop from an old player and that's built into the price, Meadows is going in the 170ish range and Braun is a post, sometimes WAY post, 200 player. Braun wins this one but let's be sure to test him for everything possible when it's over.

AUSTIN MEADOWS   THE WELSH

Former Pirates top prospect Austin Meadows now gets his full-time shot in Tampa Bay. Meadows is a nice combination of power, speed and average that is going to play as a fourth outfielder in fantasy. That might not sound exciting, but .270 15/15 isn't a bad floor. There is still a lot of upside to be had for Meadows. If Meadows would have qualified, he'd have had ranked 23rd in baseball on contact in the zone at 91.6%. Braun on the other end has been tracking backwards. He hasn't played 150 games since 2012, and averaged around 115 games the last two years. His average has also dropped three straight years. His power numbers are alright, and he steals some bases. We are bordering meh territory. To be fair, his floor at this point might be similar to Meadows with a little less average, but the continued injuries make him less and less of an attractive fantasy options. His cost is finally post 200, which makes him a guy I don't have an issue getting, but Meadows and the upside is more of what you build on. I'll take the boost in stolen bases and average for the young kid. Meadows with the 10-8 win over Braun.

★ ★ ★ WINNER - AUSTIN MEADOWS 10-9 ★ ★ ★

2019 | IN THIS LEAGUE | *Judges Scorecard*

DEREK VAN RIPER	MATT MODICA	JOE PISAPIA
MEADOWS 10-9	BRAUN 10-9	MEADOWS 10-9

Round 82: Ryan Braun vs Austin Meadows

KYLE TUCKER

VS

ODÚBEL HERRERA

	KYLE TUCKER*				ODÚBEL HERRERA
AVG.	.332 ★		AVG.		.255
HR	24 ★	ROUND	HR		22
RBI	93 ★	**83**	RBI		71
RUNS	86 ★		RUNS		64
SB	20 ★		SB		5

*2018 MiLB Stats

KYLE TUCKER

THE WELSH

Tucker hit 24 home runs and stole 20 bases in 100 Triple-A games, while also hitting .332 in 2018. He has nothing less to prove in the minors. He played 28 games in the majors and hit .141, and did literally nothing else. He has everything to prove at the major league level. Here's the rub, nothing is guaranteed for Tucker this year. The Stros signed Michael Brantley, so Tucker now would have to beat out, or get into a timeshare with Josh Reddick if he doesn't get sent to Triple-A. Another take, is Tucker could get moved. The Astros have openly said they don't want to move him in any deals, but his name has popped up every time a trade gets mentioned. The hope would be, that the commitment is for Tucker to play a huge role this year. Tucker also put on around 10 pounds of muscle in the off-season to his lean frame to pack on more power. Herrera's 20+ stolen bases seem to be a thing of the past, as Herrera has failed to steal double digit bases two straight years. A full-time Tucker season takes the easy win here, and I'll gamble with the late pick. Tucker wins 10-8.

ODÚBEL HERRERA

BOGMAN

I'm off the Odúbel Herrera bandwagon. I know that is going to make some of you sad especially because I'm supposed to be defending him here but it really looks like Herrera is primed for a giant downfall. El Torito had the highest, yes HIGHEST soft contact% of all qualified hitters. Billy Hamilton and Dee Gordon had less soft contact than Odúbel but at least he was 116/124 in hard contact%. The 22 HRs for Herrera were most likely a fluke so do not pay for them! Herrera will also be dropping from 3rd to 7th in the batting order so he'll have fewer RBI and run opportunities but hopefully more SB attempts. This doesn't sound like the defense of a player but at least he'll be in a big league lineup. Tucker isn't expected to begin the season in the bigs and the Astros have depth in the OF. Reddick has a starting spot and has been known to miss games here and there but he played 134 in 17 and 18 and he's a gold glover even if the bat isn't keeping pace. Brantley is a concern but if he starts missing games again the Astros have Marisnick, Kemp and Díaz on the roster plus Derek Fisher and Yordan Alvarez in AAA. Tucker got a shot last year, 28 games with 16 starts and he hit .140, there were only two pitchers with 70 PAs that hit worse than that! What a loser!! Don't draft anyone in this debate.

WINNER - KYLE TUCKER 10-8

2019 | *Judges Scorecard*

JAMES ANDERSON	CHRIS BLESSING	STEVE GARDNER
TUCKER KO	TUCKER 10-8	HERRERA 10-9

Round 83: Kyle Tucker vs Odúbel Herrera

NATHAN EOVALDI ⎯ VS ⎯ SHANE BIEBER

	EOVALDI		ROUND		BIEBER	
WINS	6			★ WINS	11
ERA	3.81	★	84	ERA	4.55
WHIP	1.126	★		WHIP	1.334
K	101			★ K	118
IP	111.0			★ IP	114.2

NATHAN EOVALDI   BOGMAN

I wish Eovaldi wasn't so great in the postseason because I think the draft value would be more in his favor but as it stands they are going within about 5-10 picks of each other. Shane Bieber got his buzz as a hot FA/Waiver add last season with a couple of nice months in June and August. What we can't forget though is Bieber was incredibly streaky, his monthly ERA was 6.35, 0.96, 7.33, 3.81 and 4.63 over the 5 different months he was in the bigs. Bieber was also had a weird home/road split with his home ERA at 5.88 and his road ERA at 3.56. Eovaldi had the reverse with a 2.08 ERA at home and road ERA of 5.14. One split that we have to like for Eovaldi is his ERA dropped almost a full run pitching for Boston at 3.33 versus 4.26 with TB. I know there is fear of Eovaldi going to the bullpen because he looked so good there in the World Series but the Red Sox don't have much that will push him on the roster now. The bullpen looks bad though so if he did go to the bullpen he might end up closing which would actually boost his value. We've been waiting for Eovaldi to really break out his whole career and he has a chance to do it in Boston. I'm going to the well with Eovaldi one more time, close scorecard win for him.

SHANE BIEBER   THE WELSH

Bieber fever was full in effect in Cleveland. A nine K/9 type of pitcher, with extremely low walks and an arsenal of pitches. He started his rookie season off with a very solid mid three ERA, but lost it in the second half going over five. Bieber was victim to a few big blow ups that carried that higher ERA, but he did have over a full run differential in his xFIP which was 3.30. Bieber had some Cliff Lee in him throughout the minors. It seems to be carrying over into the majors with that low walk rate, and makes him a target for 2019. Eovaldi in Boston is a solid move for him and fantasy owners. Eovaldi was better in the second half, but I question if it's going to be the big breakout move some feel it will be. Of the 12 games Eovaldi had in Boston, only three did he go six innings or more. Both guys are sitting in the general 150 draft range. Boston's overall run support makes Eovaldi a tasty fantasy option, but the innings eating, low strikeout Bieber is my choice. To get a guy that could end up returning top 100 value on his breakout campaign is a risk I'd be willing to take. Bieber with the 10-9 win

★ ★ ★ WINNER - SHANE BIEBER 10-9 ★ ★ ★

20/19 | Judges Scorecard

PAUL SPORER	EDDY ALMAGUER	JASON COLLETTE
EOVALDI 10-8	BIEBER 10-9	BIEBER 10-9

Round 84: Nathan Eovaldi vs Shane Bieber

KEN GILES **VS** JOSH HADER

	KEN GILES			JOSH HADER
SAVES	26 ★		SAVES	12
ERA	4.65	★	ERA	2.43
WHIP	1.212	★	WHIP	0.811
K	53	★	K	143
IP	50.1	★	IP	81.1

ROUND 85

KEN GILES

THE WELSH

It's interesting having someone who isn't set to log saves versus a "for sure" closer. Hader though, is one of those few relief pitchers without saves that can carry weeks for you. He led all relievers in strikeouts with 143, which was more than Jake Arrieta or Alex Wood, and only three less than Miles Mikolas. He would be a top three closer, if he just were given all the saves. That doesn't mean it won't change, and that doesn't mean he's not valuable, but he is coming at a top 100 cost. Buyer beware. I'm uncomfortable with that kind of investment. One where you'd be getting your first or second closer, and use it on a strikeout saveless reliever. Giles had a rough go in Houston, but once moved to Toronto, he ended up saving 14 of 21 games pitched. He had over a 1.30 run differential from his ERA to xFIP which is promising. His cost is also dirt cheap. He's going after José LeClerc and and Kirby Yates right now, which is nuts for a top 10 closer talent. Most of the fear probably comes from the rebuild in Toronto, and the question of opportunity. I find it easy to take the "closer" over the guy who won't collect saves. Giles in the 10-7 win.

JOSH HADER

BOGMAN

Speaking of unlikeable closers... While I don't agree with Josh Hader's Twitter takes he's still a better option than Ken Giles even if he doesn't get the full time closers job. Hader wasn't the closer for Milwaukee last season and he still wound up with 12 saves and 6 wins. 15.82 K/9 for Hader, he just has absolute filth, the dude is almost unhittable. Ken Giles actually throws harder and his K/9 has been as high as 13.98 in 2016 but it's slid since then all the way back to 9.48 last season. Hader gave up way less contact and had a higher SwStr% than Giles. The only category that Giles won last year and probably this year is saves. Hader won ERA by 2 full runs and xFIP by more than a run, WHIP by .4 and had 41 more strikeouts than Giles has ever had in his a single season. Hader is the 6th RP off the board right now and he hasn't even secured a closing job! Maybe if Giles was in a better spot for save opportunities this would be a real battle but give me Hader and don't look back.

★ ★ ★ **WINNER - JOSH HADER 10-8** ★ ★ ★

2019

In This League *Judges Scorecard*

NICK POLLACK	JAKE CIELY	CHRIS MEANEY
GILES 10-9	**HADER 10-9**	**HADER KO**

Round 85: Ken Giles vs Josh Hader

BRIAN DOZIER VS JONATHAN SCHOOP

	BRIAN DOZIER		ROUND 86		JONATHAN SCHOOP
AVG.	.215			★ AVG.	.233
HR	21			HR	21
RBI	72 ★			RBI	61
RUNS	81 ★			RUNS	61
SB	12 ★			SB	1

BRIAN DOZIER

THE WELSH

Dozier didn't do the famous "Dozier second half" parlor trick he's done every year. Stink in the first half, and then go nuts in the second. He was traded to the Dodgers, who ended up platooning him with a few players, and we started to see some kind of a slow down. Washington is a great spot for him though. He is surrounded by a surprisingly solid top to bottom lineup that is centered around great contact. My hope is it rubs off, but it'll also do two things. Get him in the lineup every day, where he was at least hitting .230 early on, and had an average of .257 in July before being moved. Number two, he should see plenty of RBI opportunities. Far more than he's had in years. Schoop actually moves to Dozier's old spot in Minnesota. He also shares very similar lower batting average and big power traits. Steamer is pretty kind to him on the average front, which could be a positive sign for his late cost. Since these two share such similar skill sets, it's easy to pick up the one big separator, stolen bases. Dozier has stolen double digit bases six straight years. Schoop has seven career stolen bases. Yes, seven in his career. Dozier had twelve last year alone. Both are bargains, but Dozier is the knockout here. Sorry Schoop for the KO.

JONATHAN SCHOOP

BOGMAN

I wish either one of these guys would have the decency to decide if they want to completely fall off or come back to provide us some value. Unbelievable similarities for these guys last year, they both were hitting terribly and were flipped at the deadline where they hit worse! Dozier's average fell 45 points to .182 with the Dodgers and Schoop feel 42 points down to .202 moving to the Brewers. The power fell off after the move for them as well, Schoop hit 17 HRs in Baltimore and 4 in Milwaukee, Dozier was 16 and 5. They both scored 16 runs with their new team and Dozier had 20 RBI with LA and Schoop had 21! Dozier fell 60 points in BABIP from 2017, Schoop feel 69 (nice)! The big difference is that Dozier steals bases and Schoop doesn't, Dozier stole 12 last year to Schoop's 1. Dozier has gone down in SB totals 3 straight seasons so we have to ask is 10ish SBs worth 50 draft spots. I don't particularly want to gamble on either but there are some good players like Desmond, Mazara and Odor going where Dozier is. I'll take my chances on Schoop later and take a better player than Dozier in the 150s.

★ ★ ★ WINNER - BRIAN DOZIER 10-9 ★ ★ ★

2019 | Judges Scorecard

STEVE GARDNER	CLAY LINK	TIM HEANEY
DOZIER 10-9	SCHOOP 10-8	DOZIER 10-8

Round 86: Brian Dozier vs Jonathan Schoop

TYLER SKAGGS VS ANDREW HEANEY

ROUND 87

	TYLER SKAGGS		ANDREW HEANEY
WINS	8	WINS	9
ERA	4.02 ★	★ ERA	4.15
WHIP	1.332	★ WHIP	1.200
K	129	★ K	180
IP	125.1	★ IP	180.0

TYLER SKAGGS

THE WELSH

Skaggs is finally coming around after being one of the centerpieces (along with Patrick Corbin) that was sent in the Dan Haren trade. Skaggs has struggled with injuries up until last year when things finally came together. The first half of the season Skaggs rocked a 2.57 ERA and struck out 105 batters in 98 innings. His last five starts were a disaster where he failed to get into the fourth inning and gave up 24 runs over that time period. He was straight fire before that though. Heaney wasn't as dominate over any stretch during the season. He also got a bit worse in the second half with a four and a half ERA. But overall was consistent across the board. Here's what I've found surprising between these two very similar young pitchers, the ADP. Heaney is a popular late 150 pick, and he's going around the 160 range. Skaggs though is sitting around 240 right now on NFBC. Injuries are being priced in. The fact that Heaney just went 180 innings this last season, and Skaggs hasn't ever gone past 125. This still doesn't quite jive with the change in cost for me. I see owning both this year, but Skaggs on value alone is an easy 10-8 win.

ANDREW HEANEY

BOGMAN

Don't blink! If you do both of these guys might not be healthy at the same time again! Heaney had TJ surgery after just one start in 2016, he game back in August of 17 and then had a shoulder issue hold him to only 5 starts. Skaggs had his TJ surgery in the middle of the 2014 campaign, came back in 2016 but only got in 10 starts, dealt with an oblique injury in 2017 that only saw him get 16 starts and then hamstring, groin and hip issues held him to 24 starts. The 24 starts were a career high, as were the 125 and a third innings but to be fair he looked really good before those injuries crept up. Skaggs had a 2.57 ERA at the break but the 2nd half he just couldn't get right after the first two starts he didn't get out of the 4th inning in his last 5 starts before they shut him down for good. Heaney looked like a typical pitcher in the 2nd season removed from TJ surgery, he showed way more control than in his few 2017 starts, he threw his slider way more often too. Heaney did start 30 games, which Skaggs has never done and while his ERA rose in the 2nd half he didn't get shut down and this was his first full season in the bigs. I might not take Heaney where he's going but Skaggs is a spot starter unless you're in a deep league.

WINNER - ANDREW HEANEY 10-9

2019 Judges Scorecard

IN THIS LEAGUE

EDDY ALMAGUER	RYAN BLOOMFIELD	SAMMY REID
SKAGGS 10-9	HEANEY 10-8	DRAW

Round 87: Tyler Skaggs vs Andrew Heaney

NICK SENZEL VS PAUL DEJONG

	NICK SENZEL		ROUND		PAUL DEJONG	
AVG.	.310 ★				AVG.	.241
HR	6		**88**	★	HR	19
RBI	25			★	RBI	68
RUNS	23			★	RUNS	68
SB	8 ★				SB	1

*2018 MiLB Stats

NICK SENZEL

THE WELSH

What are you willing to risk to get that next big prospect? We've talked about guys like Eloy Jimenez and Peter Alonso who have no guarantees versus players that are up now. Senzel is the next in line. Compared to the other two, he might be the best mix of everything you want. Multi-position capable, plus a higher batting average and a perfect combo of power and speed. Currently the Reds are talking about him being their center fielder with Billy Hamilton out of town. He missed a lot of time last year, which may hurt his chances in spring training, but he won't be down for long. Steamer projects him around 60 games, and I feel ok doubling that. I'd feel confident banking on 15/15 .275 average year on the low end. I won't speculate on the RBI/RUN totals without knowing where he is hitting, but hitting five in the lineup would suit him. DeJong is coming off a fractured hand. He's failed to reach 120 games in both of his MLB seasons. He also saw his average dip from the .285 down to .241. He's in a fantastic spot in the lineup right now, and if he can stay healthy, he could be a three category guy. He doesn't steal and his average is a big question. Both are cheap, but as we've seen, it's not often you can get a prospect that should see most of the season past the 200th pick. Senzel in a very close 10-9 win.

PAUL DEJONG

BOGMAN

I want to take Senzel in this debate but the Reds OF situation is scaring me off. I know that Nick Senzel is a 3B but Eugenio Suárez has played at least 143 games the last 3 seasons and he's gotten better every year so that's just not an option right now. The plan for the Reds is to play Senzel in CF in Spring Training and the minors with the hopes that he replaces Billy Hamilton there at some point. The Reds already have 4 OF for 3 spots as we've discussed previously in Schebler, Kemp, Puig and Winker. I'm not the biggest fan of DeJong, he didn't hit lefties last year (.198 average), he sank a bit in the 2nd half and his HR/FB ratio fell over 6% from 2017. However, DeJong did increase his contact%, made more hard contact, less soft contact and lowered his SwStr%. DeJong's BABIP fell way off from .349 to .288 last season which explains the lower average, so he's probably not the .285 hitter he was in 2017 but probably not all the way down to .241 last year I'd guess about .260ish. DeJong also gets the coveted spot of batting in front of new Cards acquisition Paul Goldschmidt and might see some better pitches to hack at. Senzel is a better player but I don't see where the ABs come from. Give me DeJong in a tight one 10-9.

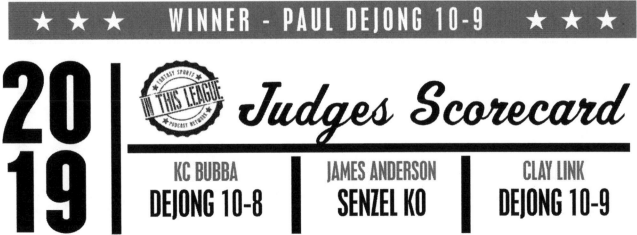

★ ★ ★ WINNER - PAUL DEJONG 10-9 ★ ★ ★

2019 Judges Scorecard

IN THIS LEAGUE

KC BUBBA	JAMES ANDERSON	CLAY LINK
DEJONG 10-8	SENZEL KO	DEJONG 10-9

Round 88: Nick Senzel vs Paul DeJong

JAKE LAMB VS KYLE SEAGER

	JAKE LAMB			ROUND		KYLE SEAGER	
AVG.	.222	★				AVG.	.221
HR	6			**89**	★	HR	22
RBI	31				★	RBI	78
RUNS	34				★	RUNS	62
SB	1				★	SB	2

JAKE LAMB

BOGMAN

I think we've been talking about these two guys for 3 straight years. In 2017 we didn't want to buy Seager coming off of that big 30 HR year and Lamb was the better deal, in 2018 it was the reverse as Lamb had his 30 HR season and this year they both are going after pick 200! They both have unbelievably bad splits, Jake Lamb can't hit lefties. In 356 ABs against lefties he's hitting .160 against them, in comparison Patrick Corbin, a left-handed pitcher, hits .156 against lefties. Seager has hit righties decently in his career as he's not much of an average hitter but in 2018 he only hit .208 against them. Lamb is more futile but way more ABs are going to come off of righties than lefties of which Lamb hits .269 for his career. Lamb also has room for improvement after coming off of shoulder surgery that shut him down after only 56 games. The initial injury happened on Opening Day so he drug it around for the full season. Seager has gone down in batting average, BB%, BABIP, HR/FB, OPS and up in SwStr% for 3 straight seasons. The good news about both is that this is a sub 200 pick at this point for most leagues but it's still Seager going about 30-50 picks ahead of Lamb. I would take Lamb and the upside even if they were even in the draft. Scorecard win for Lamb!

KYLE SEAGER

THE WELSH

Boy do we love pairing these two together, right? So goes one, so goes the other it seems. Lamb is being asked to fill the Goldy role and move into first base. Though Lamb can't hit lefties at all, the previous two season before last, he had been essentially a 30 home run, 85 Run, 95 RBI third baseman. Injuries destroyed his season last year. The offense won't be the same, but he should be hitting between four and five. Seager is on a three year production drop on almost every front. Home runs, average, runs, RBI, BABIP, walk percentage all dropped, while his strikeouts keep rising. Regardless of the dips, Seager is a still steady eddy. Your floor is 24 home runs, 70 runs, 80 RBI and a .240 average. His floor is probably higher than Lamb, but the upside is with the hitter friendly park Lamb hits in. They are both going post 200, but Lamb is criminally undervalued right now. NFBC he sits around 280. I wouldn't be expecting .270 and 35 home runs, but I don't think we are far off from another 30 home run season. Lamb takes three of five categories and a 10-8 win over Seager.

★ ★ ★ WINNER - KYLE SEAGER 10-9 ★ ★ ★

20 19

IN THIS LEAGUE

Judges Scorecard

DEREK VAN RIPER	ALEX CHAMBERLAIN	JAKE CIELY
SEAGER 10-9	SEAGER 10-9	SEAGER 10-9

Round 89: Jake Lamb vs Kyle Seager

RICK PORCELLO VS JAKE ARRIETA

RICK PORCELLO

WINS 17 ★
ERA 4.28
WHIP 1.176 ★
K 190 ★
IP 191.1 ★

ROUND 90

JAKE ARRIETA

WINS 10
★ **ERA** 3.96
WHIP 1.286
K 138
IP 172.2

RICK PORCELLO

BOGMAN

This one is all about Wins. Wins of course can be finicky and a lot of people will say not to chase them but they are one of the 5 stats we are looking for from pitchers and Porcello gets them. 50 of them in the last 3 seasons for Porcello, Arrieta is no slouch as he has 48 but his totals have gone down for 3 consecutive seasons. Situation of course plays a huge role in getting wins as we know from watching Jacob deGrom last year. The Phillies are a rising club and have added some pieces and will probably keep looking to build but the Red Sox just came off a season where they had the best record and won the World Series! The only one of the categories that Porcello didn't win between these two last season was ERA but he did win xFIP! Arietta dropped his K/9 to 7.19, his lowest since 2013 and Porcello raised his to a career high 8.94 with another career high 190 strikeouts. Porcello is just the better pitcher, he's in the better position to earn a Win and he's in his early 30's not mid 30's like Arrieta. His draft price is more expensive because he's better, you want to start him out because over the last 3 years he gives you a better than 50% chance to get a W and very few pitchers can say that. This is not a KO because Arrieta is almost free but it's an easy 10-7 win.

JAKE ARRIETA

THE WELSH

Arrieta is on a four year decrease in production. His rise in home runs isn't great being in Philly, and the strikeouts falling to under 7.50 K/9 limits some of the value, regardless of wins. His value is at an all-time low. What's really interesting is the velocity increases he saw on his fastball from 92.1 to 93 and his cutter from 87.8 to 89.4, yet he had his lowest swinging strike rate since 2012. The biggest change seems to be a declining usage in his curveball, and an uptick on his changeup. He doesn't have great separation between his fastball/cutter, and his changeup velocity can't be helping. Maybe with a arsenal adjustment we could see some adjusted results? His June was awful, but there were two really dominate months mixed with a third very solid month. Those months combined equaled a sub three ERA. Something I wonder if the Phillies address, is how he falls apart on the third go around. He had a three and a half ERA thru the first two turns in the order, but jumped to over five on the third. Limiting his innings could help, but he proved to be able to go deep in key situations. Porcello himself was pretty solid. Though never displaying any dominate stints, he was pretty even the whole year. He is a better strikeout option at this point, and more trustworthy for wins. Arrieta can't win this more than 10-9 without a major shift in his approach, but I do think it's possible with what we've seen before. He's also 50+ picks cheaper. This is almost a draw!

★ ★ ★ WINNER - RICK PORCELLO 10-9 ★ ★ ★

2019

In This League *Judges Scorecard*

ROB SILVER
PORCELLO 10-9

NATE GRIMM
ARRIETA 10-8

MATT MODICA
PORCELLO 10-9

Round 90: Rick Porcello vs Jake Arrieta

ADAM JONES VS MANUEL MARGOT

	ADAM JONES			ROUND	MANUEL MARGOT	
AVG.	.281	★		**91**	AVG.	.245
HR	15	★			HR	8
RBI	63	★			RBI	51
RUNS	54	★			RUNS	50
SB	7			★	SB	11

ADAM JONES

BOGMAN

Let's make excuses for the 2018 performances of these guys! It's actually the same one for both of them, they both injured their wrists in May and the power wasn't the same as it usually is. These guys have bigger issues as it stands right now, Adam Jones doesn't have a job and Margot is a platoon player. Adam Jones will sign somewhere and wherever that is it has to be a better situation than it was in Baltimore. Even in the basement dwelling Charm City Jones 5 year lows excluding 2018 were .265 average, 74 runs, 26 HRs, and 73 RBI. Margot has a chance to earn back more playing time with a good performance in Spring Training but Renfroe, Cordero and Reyes can all earn time with good looks in ST for the Padres. Margot is one of the few players that should be hitting the ball on the ground more than in the air. His average was 18 points higher in 2017 and he hit the ball on the ground just 2.5% more and made way less hard contact. The ballpark isn't doing Margot any favors either, he hit .217 at home and .271 on the road in 2018. Jones hit a little bit better at home than on the road in his career but his away average is still better than Margot's career average. Adam Jones just needs a home and it doesn't really matter where it is and he wins this debate. Let someone else take Margot and drop him after a month.

MANUEL MARGOT

THE WELSH

Remember when Manny Margot was the hot sleeper pick? I Wish I didn't! Margot went in the wrong direction last year. Margot was thought to be someone who would be a plus average hitter, but he went from a .260 to .240 hitter. What I want to bank on this year, is he gets back to what got him here. Last year he looked to be trying to hit more home runs than ever. He pulled the ball 12% more than the previous season, which is a huge rise. His hard hit percentage jumped from 25.4% to 39.3%, but because he was trying to pull it for power, he stopped using all of the field. That is just not his game. His cut in strikeouts was a positive sign. If he can just get back to using the whole field, he's got a chance to do some damage. This is me being hopeful this change can happen, which I will bank on this year. Adam Jones isn't the same Adam Jones we are used to, but he's essentially floor Margot with a little more power, average and less stolen bases. Jones has to hit, as he won't get on base with that under four percent walk rate. As of writing this we are waiting to see what type of gig he gets in 2019. I think both are solid cheap options, but I believe Jones' production is replaceable, where the stolen base and semi-power potential Margot provides is few and far between around pick 250. Margot with a 10-9 win.

★ ★ ★ WINNER - MANUEL MARGOT 10-8 ★ ★ ★

2019 — Judges Scorecard

JOE PISAPIA	PAUL SPORER	CHRIS MEANEY
MARGOT 10-7	MARGOT 10-9	JONES 10-9

Round 91: Adam Jones vs Manuel Margot

JOSH JAMES VS MIKE SOROKA

	JOSH JAMES			ROUND			MIKE SOROKA	
WINS	2			**92**		WINS	2	
ERA	2.35	★				ERA	3.51	
WHIP	0.957	★				WHIP	1.442	
K	29	★				K	21	
IP	23.0				★	IP	25.2	

JOSH JAMES
BOGMAN

I don't like to get on too many hype machines but I'll go ahead and jump on the one for Josh James. It's crazy what some good sleep can do for you as Josh James saw his velocity tick way up when he started using a CPAP machine for his sleep apnea a few years ago. Josh's fastball sat at 97.1 in his 23 innings in the bigs last season. James only saw 3 starts and 3 relief appearances but his K/9 was stayed over 11 and his SwStr% was the exact same in the bigs as it was in AAA at 14.3%. He gets a chance to prove it at the big league level this year as he's going to stay with Astros for the long haul after the losses of Keuchel and Morton. Someone in the Houston rotation is just keeping the seat warm for Forrest Whitley but that looks like Framber Valdez or whomever wins the #5 spot in the rotation. Soroka got a midseason call to the bigs and looked pretty good in 5 starts, he had a respectable K/9 of 7.36, didn't walk many and had a very mid 3's ERA. Unfortunately Soroka was shut down with some shoulder issues in late June but, he pitched in fall instructs with no pain and should be fine for the spring. Soroka has to win a job in the rotation between him, Touki, Newcomb, Wright, Gohara, Allard and Fried they have 3 spots. 1st round KO on the James hype train!

MIKE SOROKA
THE WELSH

Both pitchers are currently lined up for a rotation spot with their team, but neither may be guaranteed that spot for the season. If the Braves brought someone in it could bump Soroka. The Astros already brought in Wade Miley, which pushes James to the fifth pitcher in the rotation. James came on the scene in a big way this previous year. The biggest advantage I'd give him are his potentially elite strikeout numbers. His control could be an issue, though his short stint in the majors ended up being solid. He's a very popular sleeper pick this year, but I have some reservations. Soroka, though younger, is the better pitcher. Though James has an electric fastball right now, I think Soroka's pitch mix with control is better suited for longer sustainability in the majors. If one of these guys was to lose their spot due to performance it is without question Josh James in my eyes. The Astros haven't been afraid to put young pitchers in their bullpen ala Francis Martes. Whitley is also the guy breathing down his neck. Soroka has his fair share in the likes of Touki, Wright and Gohara, but at an almost 100 spot difference in drafts, I think Soroka is the type of guy that pulls 140 solid innings of sub four ERA and double digit wins together. James is going around 200, so not a crazy investment, but outside of strikeouts, I believe more of a risk if you are counting on season long production. They are still close, but Soroka with a 10-9 decision.

★ ★ ★ WINNER - MIKE SOROKA 10-9 ★ ★ ★

2019 | *Judges Scorecard*

JASON COLLETTE	EDDY ALMAGUER	CHRIS BLESSING
DRAW	**JAMES 10-9**	**SOROKA 10-8**

Round 92: Josh James vs Mike Soroka

ANDREW MILLER VS KIRBY YATES

	ANDREW MILLER		ROUND 93		KIRBY YATES
SAVES	2			★ SAVES	12
ERA	4.24			★ ERA	2.14
WHIP	1.382			★ WHIP	0.921
K	45			★ K	90
IP	34.0			★ IP	63.0

ANDREW MILLER

THE WELSH

I am a big Andrew Miller guy. The fastball slider combo can be lethal, as seen in 2017. 2018 was a different story, as he got less swinging strikes and gave up more home runs. In fact, he gave up 16 home runs in only 34 innings, where he gave up 21 in 62.2 the year before. The move to the NL and with the Cardinals has me excited. He isn't guaranteed to be the only closer, but should see plenty of saves. The team has said they will use him in high leverage situations, which could mean the 7th, but I am banking on his experience being the thing the Cards go to for the majority of save chances in 2019. Yates saw solid success last year in which he added a split finger fastball to his arsenal. I actually think Yates is a solid option if he closes the whole year. I don't know if that's a guarantee or not. There are some bullpen arms out there that could change up the closer role. His cost sits in the 120 draft range, which isn't for me with some of the floating uncertainty. Andrew Miller though, is going post 250, because the Cards haven't named a closer yet. I will probably own a lot of shares of Miller this year. He's one of those guys with the high strikeouts that helps you even when not saving games. He was Josh Hader two or three years ago. Yates closing all season might flip this, but I am going to say 10-8 in favor of Miller.

KIRBY YATES

BOGMAN

I actually like both of these guys. Kirby Yates took over when the Padres traded Brad Hand to Cleveland and didn't relinquish the job. The Padres even saw significant interest in Yates and decided to hold onto him instead of flipping him for something at the deadline. Yates really has put together two great seasons in San Diego 2018 was easily his best with career bests in Saves, ERA, WHIP, Ks, Wins, HR/9 and BB/9. While the Padres aren't expected to blow the world away in save opportunities Yates will be their guy in the 9th. The reason Brad Hand was flipped to Cleveland was because Cody Allen kept giving games away and Andrew Miller couldn't stay healthy. Miller threw his fewest amount of innings since his 2010 season in Miami due to hamstring, knee and shoulder issues throughout the 2018 season. Before Miller's injury plagued 2018 he had a K/9 over 13, ERA under 2 and WHIP under one in consecutive seasons. St. Louis is a GREAT landing spot for Miller as they had all kinds of issues with the bullpen last season. However, it looks like Jordan Hicks settled into the closers role and will get the first crack at it. Should Hicks falter Miller will most likely get first crack. My money is on Yates for the saves but I don't mind taking Miller because he's almost free. 10-9 in Yates' favor.

★ ★ ★ WINNER - KIRBY YATES 10-7 ★ ★ ★

20 19

Judges Scorecard

IN THIS LEAGUE — FANTASY SPORTS PODCAST NETWORK

NICK POLLACK	NATE GRIMM	STEVE GARDNER
YATES 10-8	YATES KO	YATES 10-8

Round 93: Andrew Miller vs Kirby Yates

JORGE POLANCO VS LUIS URIAS

ROUND 94

	JORGE POLANCO		LUIS URIAS	
AVG.	.288	★ AVG.	.296	
HR	6	★ HR	8	
RBI	42	★ RBI	45	
RUNS	38	★ RUNS	83	
SB	7 ★	SB	2	

*2018 MiLB Stats

*

JORGE POLANCO

BOGMAN

This is value city right here. Jorge Polanco only played half of the season because he was exposed as a cheater with a positive PED test right before the season started. Even with the suspension he still finished at a great pace over the back half of the season. Polanco is slated to hit leadoff for the Twins this season and while he only started 5 games there in 18' he did hit .409 there over 22 ABs so there is some room for improvement in average and runs. Polanco could pace out with more SBs at the top of the lineup too, he's had as many as 20 in a season in 2015 over 3 levels. Urias will get his first chance at a full year of big league ABs hitting 2nd for the Padres. Urias got a taste at the end of last season and he could only muster a .208 average with 2 bombs and a swipe. While not being a power or speed guy Urias has hit very well in his minor league career, he hit .296 in AA in 17 and the same .296 in AAA last year so it looks like the average should climb up. Urias also had a .398 OBP in those last two minor league seasons as well so combining that with hitting in the top 3rd of the order should add up to a decent year for him. I'll take the chance for a 15-15 season with Polanco in this one but Urias can still provide useful should he be more successful than his 2018 cup of coffee.

LUIS URIAS

THE WELSH

Regardless of Urias' first stint in the pros, he is a very polished high average hitter, who will also excel in OBP leagues. He's a smaller guy, but thick frame. He doesn't run a ton, but could very easily steal you 10-12 bases. There is some real power in there, but we don't know how it will develop. He makes such good contact, I wouldn't doubt a 15-18 home run year either. This season he's going to be given a chance to play everyday. It may start at short, but it could end at second base pending what the team does with Fernando Tatis Jr. Projected depth charts show Urias hitting two, which is right in line with his skill set. I'm not trying to bury projections just on Urias after we've used them all over the book, but I don't know if projections know how to tackle him, especially when they project him with a sub .250 average. High runs, high average and an open question as to where his power and RBI's go, make Urias an intriguing late option. He's going post 300, so essentially undrafted in most places. Polanco is kind of a forgotten guy as well, with an low return power/speed combo, while also having a decent contribution in the run and RBI department. He's costing you around a pick around 200. I'd love to come back and look at this at this one at the end of the year, because I could see Urias taking every category but stolen bases. Urias with a 10-8 win.

★ ★ ★ WINNER - JORGE POLANCO 10-9 ★ ★ ★

20 19

IN THIS LEAGUE

Judges Scorecard

JAMES ANDERSON	RYAN BLOOMFIELD	TIM HEANEY
URIAS KO	POLANCO 10-7	POLANCO 10-8

Round 94: Jorge Polanco vs Luis Urias

JED LOWRIE VS DJ LEMAHIEU

	JED LOWRIE						DJ LEMAHIEU	
AVG.	.267			**ROUND**		★ AVG.	.276	
HR	23	★		**95**		HR	15	
RBI	99	★				RBI	62	
RUNS	78					★ RUNS	90	
SB	0					★ SB	6	

JED LOWRIE

BOGMAN

I'm at a loss to explain why DJ is going ahead of Lowrie. I LOVE the Yankees lineup but hitting 9th for the Yankees is not hitting 1st or 2nd for the Rockies which is where Lemahieu took all of his ABs outside of pinch hitting last season. LeMahieu also hit .229 away from Coors Field last season and his career average drops to .264 on the road while it was .330 in Coors. LeMahieu loses his cushy home ballpark and drops to the bottom of the lineup. Jed Lowrie goes to the Mets and will hit in the same spot with them as he did with the A's, 2nd. Lowrie got better on the road to the tune of .284 while hitting .250 in the Coliseum. Lowrie and LeMahieu had career highs in HRs last year (23 and 15), they were both weirdly better on the road with the power 19 for Lowrie and 11 for LeMahieu. The only reason that I see for LeMahieu to win this battle is because Lowrie hasn't been able to stay healthy over the course of his career. Before 2017 Lowrie had only played over 100 games in 2 of 9 big league seasons but, he has played 153+ two years in a row. If LeMahieu moves up in the lineup in New York this would be more of a debate but I would still take Lowrie due to LeMahieu's hitting outside of Colorado. More power, higher in the lineup and cheaper draft price. Lowrie early round KO.

DJ LEMAHIEU

THE WELSH

Welcome to New York, guys! Jed's advantage starts with the full-time roll. It looks like Lowrie is going to be the third baseman for the Mets. Lowrie was the talk of the town in the first half with his .285 average and 16 home runs. He fell off hard though, hitting only .239 with a drop to seven home runs. His power seemed real, but the solid contact isn't a lock. DJ LeMahieu is built on solid contact. He had a dip on his average and BABIP this past year, but hit a career high 15 home runs in only 128 games. I know it's Colorado, but New York isn't some pitcher friendly park by any means. DJ is not currently locked into a guaranteed role. Things could change easy, though. Early Depth charts have DJ at second base hitting nine. The team also brought in Tulowitzki, who could play SS and move Gleyber to second base. He might end up a super utility guy, which isn't the worst thing, but it limits the opportunity that Lowrie might have. Regardless of playing time, I see DJ winning this 3-2 as far as categories go. Runs will be close, but I give him the edge, plus average and stolen bases are a lock for me. Both are post 200 drafted players, so give me the versatile LeMahieu in a 10-9 win.

★ ★ ★ **WINNER - JED LOWRIE 10-8** ★ ★ ★

20 19 | *Judges Scorecard*

IN THIS LEAGUE

JOE PISAPIA	MATT MODICA	PAUL SPORER
LOWRIE 10-7	LOWRIE 10-8	LOWRIE 10-8

Round 95: Jed Lowrie vs DJ LeMahieu

ALEX WOOD vs NICK PIVETTA

ALEX WOOD

WINS	9	★
ERA	3.68	★
WHIP	1.207	★
K	135	
IP	151.2	

ROUND 96

NICK PIVETTA

WINS	7	
ERA	4.77	
WHIP	1.305	
K	188	★
IP	164.0	★

ALEX WOOD
BOGMAN

I get the excitement of Pivetta, young pitcher with high K upside and a nice xFIP could mean big things. Pivetta switched the pitch mix a little bit, throwing the curveball about 7% more often than he did in 17 and the ERA dropped almost a run and a half, the WHIP dropped by .21 and his K/9 went up almost a full strikeout! The Phillies have been adding to the roster too so there could be an influx in run support so the 7-14 record improves. The league seemed to figure out his pitch mix though, after a stellar 2 month beginning of the season Pivetta had ERAs of 7.71 in June, 5.40 July, 4.05 August and 5.48 in September. Alex Wood is going 50 spots later and he beat Pivetta in everything but Ks last season. He was traded to Cincinnati and will be bringing back his windup that he used in 2017 when he had a career best 2.72 ERA and 16 wins. Steamer has him for an ERA over 4 but I don't that's right, he's never had an ERA over 3.84 and his home/road career splits at 3.10 to 3.47. The Dodgers tend to baby their pitchers so this could actually end up being a great move for Wood. Give me Wood (phrasing) 50 picks later and I'll take the risk on Darvish where Pivetta is going.

NICK PIVETTA
THE WELSH

Pivetta's 2018 created the makings of a breakout pitcher. 10+ K/9, under three B/9 and more than a run lower xFIP than his ERA. He was one of only 13 starting pitchers with over 160 innings to average that 10+ K/9. The good goes with the bad though, as his ERA was almost five. In fact, from June on he only had one month with an ERA under five. He's still giving up too many home runs, pitched to a .300+ BABIP and his ERA doubled once he got to the second half of the order. If we were aggregating a top 10 sleeper list from around the industry, I almost guarantee Pivetta would be on that list. If his xFIP was his ERA, we would be talking about a top 30 pitcher in fantasy. This is why he won't come cheap. Alex Wood is actually a positive floor version of Pivetta this year. Wood doesn't shine on strikeouts, but is a solid middle of the rotation guy that maintains his ERA. His move to Cincinnati though, could result in a rise on that ERA. Wood dominates lefties. Fun fact, Wood gave up 14 homers last year, all were to righties. Wood's health comes into play as well, as even Steamer projects Wood for about 30 less innings than Pivetta this season. I wish Pivetta's ADP was lower, as wood is in the 200 range, while Pivetta is around 150, but Pivetta is a few adjustments away from a full fledged breakout, and he's more than worth that 150 spot. Pivetta with the KO.

★ ★ ★ WINNER - NICK PIVETTA 10-8 ★ ★ ★

20 19 | Judges Scorecard

ALEX CHAMBERLAIN	SAMMY REID	JASON COLLETTE
PIVETTA 10-8	PIVETTA 10-7	PIVETTA 10-8

Round 96: Alex Wood vs Nick Pivetta

JACKIE
BRADLEY JR.

VS

ADAM
EATON

				ROUND			
AVG.	.234			**97**	★	AVG.	.301
HR	13	★				HR	5
RBI	59	★				RBI	33
RUNS	76	★				RUNS	55
SB	17	★				SB	9

JACKIE BRADLEY JR.

THE WELSH

The ALCS MVP certainly raised his value in the final months of the season. He hit .213 in the first half and .269 in the second, while hitting one more homer in almost 30 less games. He hit the ball harder, and pulled it more, but still hit for a three year low average. He and fantasy owners have been chasing that 2016 season where he hit 26 home runs. It looks like we aren't getting back to that place. On a positive note, where he doesn't help in one spot, he is helping in others. He had a career high in stolen bases, and got his runs back up. If he can adjust to making more contact and lower the strikeout rate, he'll find solid value again. He's got second half momentum on his side. Adam Eaton is a solid source of average, but outside of that, there just isn't much else to trust. He isn't a source of RBI's, but if he stays on the field, you can count on runs. He should have a starting gig, assuming Harper or another free agent aren't signed. He's only played a combined 118 games the last two years, so he isn't a slam dunk. Eaton is a safer roto play, but is extremely limited on upside. It's almost to the point of why bother with him. I'll take the discount I get with JBJ, but I don't need it. This is a 10-7 win for Junior.

ADAM EATON

BOGMAN

Adam Eaton has really only one flaw and that is staying on the field. Eaton has a little pop, steals a few bases, has a career OBP over .360 and career batting average of .287. Eaton has no crazy splits over his career either, he hits righties 11 points better than lefties, hits 8 points better on the road and he likes the 2nd half as he is over .300 there (and has more ABs than in the 1st half). It's simple when Eaton plays he performs and he's going to hit leadoff for the Nationals this season for as many games as he can. Bradley is flawed, he has more power and speed than Eaton but his career batting average is almost 50 points lower than Eaton's. Bradley's career contact rate is over 11% lower than Adam Eaton and he was 127 of 140 in contact% last season among qualifiers. The answer here might be to try take Jorge Polanco or Josh James where Eaton is going and then take Adam Jones or Ketel Marte where Bradley is going. If this was a real boxing match Bradley wouldn't connect on enough punches and Eaton would gas out half way through. I'll take Eaton and hope he stays healthy between them.

★ ★ ★ WINNER - JACKIE BRADLEY JR. 10-8 ★ ★ ★

20
19

Judges Scorecard

IN THIS LEAGUE
FANTASY SPORTS
PODCAST NETWORK

ROB SILVER	NATE GRIMM	KC BUBBA
BRADLEY 10-9	**EATON 10-8**	**BRADLEY KO**

Round 97: Jackie Bradley Jr. vs Adam Eaton

FORREST WHITLEY VS JESUS LUZARDO

	FORREST WHITLEY	ROUND 98	JESUS LUZARDO	
WINS	0		WINS	10
ERA	3.76		ERA	2.88
WHIP	0.987		WHIP	1.088
K	34		K	129
IP	26.1		IP	109.1

*2018 MiLB Stats

*2018 MiLB Stats

FORREST WHITLEY

BOGMAN

Taking either one of these guys is dicey and I don't really like drafting someone I know that I'll have to wait on for either an injury or the big league team to give up on the guy ahead of him. These two both have sexy upside but very, very little experience even in the minors. Luzardo got to AAA for 4 starts last season and was shelled after owning AA his ERA jumped from 2.29 in AA to 7.31 over those last 4 AAA starts. Whitley didn't even hit AAA most likely because he was suspended 50 games for violating the minor league drug policy. The opportunity is there for both in 2019 though. The A's really need a good starter, Cotton is still recovering from TJ surgery, Manea will probably miss the whole season with shoulder surgery and the current rotation is Fiers, Mengden, Montas, Bassitt and Brooks... yikes. The problem there is if the A's are not winning at all early in the season they may have no incentive to start Luzardo's service time. My fear for Whitley is that the Astro's limit his innings at the end of the season to save him for the playoffs. They could also stash Whitley in the bullpen if they want to go with the 4 man rotation of Verlander, Cole, McHugh and James OR trade him to get another starter. These are ballsy picks, give me Whitley with the hope the Astros need a starter to get to the playoffs.

JESUS LUZARDO

THE WELSH

These are the two best pitching prospects in the game right here. Whitley is a force as he blows it by hitters with a devastating fastball, curveball, slider combo. From what I've seen in person, he can get hit early a bit, but once he settles in, good luck. His biggest question, like Luzardo, is opportunity. Luzardo controls the batter, where Whitley over powers. Luzardo's control, along with pitch mix and ability to change his delivery, makes him a really advanced young pitcher. Ok, they're both good, we get it. So this all comes down to which team will commit. I am fascinated by projections with these two, which have been right at 92 innings (Steamer). I think Whitley will actually find a harder time cracking the Astros rotation, not due to talent, but more that the Astros may not need to push him in the lineup. There are also service time considerations. We saw something similar with Kyle Tucker with the Astros, and they did just sign Wade Miley. The A's may actually give Luzardo a shot to crack the rotation in spring, but I have my doubts this happens. Long term, Whitley has the makings of an elite fantasy starting pitcher, and would be my choice in dynasty, but for 2019, give me Luzardo. A 10-8 win.

★ ★ ★ WINNER - JESUS LUZARDO 10-8 ★ ★ ★

20 19 Judges Scorecard

JAMES ANDERSON	EDDY ALMAGUER	CHRIS BLESSING
LUZARDO 10-7	WHITLEY 10-8	LUZARDO 10-9

Round 98: Forrest Whitley Jr. vs Jesus Luzardo

WILLY ADAMES VS AMED ROSARIO

	WILLY ADAMES				AMED ROSARIO
AVG.	.278	★		AVG.	.256
HR	10	★		HR	9
RBI	34		★	RBI	51
RUNS	43		★	RUNS	76
SB	6		★	SB	24

ROUND 99

WILLY ADAMES

BOGMAN

I get chasing steals with Rosario, it looks like a decent deal around pick 175-200 why not grab him and see what he can do. Rosario isn't an inept hitter, he'll hit in the .245-.260ish range and he has a little pop. The problem he has is that he doesn't get on base to hit at the top of the lineup, he's been under .300 OBP for his two big league seasons so far. Last season when the Mets were going through all kinds of injuries and didn't have great bats they let Rosario hit leadoff and that's where 16 of those 24 swipes came from. Now that the Mets have added Lowrie, Cano and Ramos there's no more room for Rosario at the top of that lineup. The SBs won't go away completely for him but it's doubtful that he hits that number again. Willy Adames doesn't have the speed that Rosario does and he's going to hit 7 for Tampa just like Rosario is in New York but he has a chance to move up in the order. Kiermaier, while an amazing fielder, saw his OBP plunge to a career low .282 last year while Adames was at .348 in his 85 games last year. Adames also hit .318 in August and .341 in September and was really getting rolling at the end of the season. Give me they guy with a little more pop, better OBP and a chance to move up in the lineup over the one trick pony. Adames in a scorecard win!

AMED ROSARIO

THE WELSH

This was our ITL Captains write-in debate, voted by the highest supporters in our ITL Army. No surprise to see to very highly rated shortstops, who haven't lived up to the hype, yet get the vote. There is a lot I like about Adames this year. I think he's going to tap into his power this coming season, he'll steal a handful of bases and at least hit above .250 to make him a sleeper shortstop in deeper leagues. The thing that sets Rosario apart are those stolen bases. He is weighed heavy on his second half, as he stole 18 of his 24 in the final 63 games of the year. I worry a little as 16 of those came from the leadoff spot, and it looks as if he'll be hitting toward the bottom of the order. I don't know if it was about aggression at the leadoff spot, or he was given the green light at any spot, but it's something to monitor. Regardless though, if they are a few spots off on power numbers, average isn't a separator, Rosario's stolen bases set him firmly apart. A 10 home run 25 stolen base season might be a floor for the young shortstop, and gives him an easy 10-8 win.

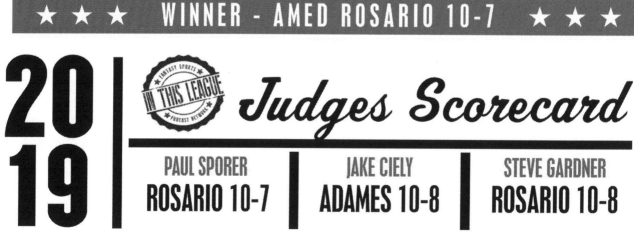

★ ★ ★ **WINNER - AMED ROSARIO 10-7** ★ ★ ★

20 19

Judges Scorecard

PAUL SPORER	JAKE CIELY	STEVE GARDNER
ROSARIO 10-7	ADAMES 10-8	ROSARIO 10-8

Round 99: Willy Adames vs Amed Rosario

Five from Last Year

TREVOR STORY <u>VS</u> JAVIER BAEZ

2018

Bogman's Take:

Looks like we were both right on this one last year! Báez wound up as a first round pick blowing away expectations hitting career highs in everything AND ditto for Story. Báez did it hitting all over the lineup, he spent at least 4 games at every spot in the order for the Cubs. Báez also played 90 games at 2B, 64 at SS and 20 at 3B. Story played all 156 games at SS and spent 142 of those games at either 4th or 5th in the lineup. Our judges were split in this one as well with two 10-9 scores for each and one 10-8 for Báez. Looks like these guys are here to stay. If I had to pick one from the 2019 issue to compare to this it would be Moncada vs Hampson. Both of those guys have huge upside but are unproven.

Welsh's Take:

It's fascinating reading back as I said "Story isn't going to steal bases" and the guy steals 27. I did say I wouldn't be surprised if Story found a happy medium with his production, but he found way more than that. I think I nailed a lot of my argument which was, he is already doing the work, he just needs a full go, which he got. Báez is a dynamic hitter, and he did it on all fronts. No judge was wrong if you think about it, since it was a really close debate. Story won the debate, but Báez took a small lead, so win for Clay Link and myself. This is also a great example of how you can approach these debates, that it isn't that one guy can't also be great, and there has to be one clear cut winner, but with the right argument sometimes the guys that are right in line of a breakout, can do it together. It won't always work out like this, but between the write-ups, the cost and judges close decisions, this debate shined from our 2018 book. If I had to pick a debate from this years 2019 to mirror the Story/Báez debate that we look back on to see mutal dual returns, I am going to pick Mallex Smith and Billy Hamilton. Stolen Bases will carry such huge value, and both guys could be 50+. It's not the same as far as complete players, but value wise, both guys could have big 2019's that we look back on and laugh.

2018 Judges
Vlad Sedler - Story 10-8
Clay Link - Baez 10-9
Nate Grimm - Story 10-9

WINNER
Trevor Story in a 10-9 Win

TREVOR BAUER VS COLE HAMELS
2018

Bogman's Take:

Put these two together from last year and you have a really great season. Bauer would have been the clear cut winner, lowering his ERA from the 4+ in every season he's pitched (starting in 2012) to 2.21. Hamels was great with the Cubs, 8 of his 12 starts with the Cubs were quality and his ERA dropped from 4.72 with Texas to 2.36 with Chicago. Bauer went on the DL in mid-August right when Hamels was taking off for the Cubbies. It's possible that people were able to replace Bauer with Hamels late in the season because he really got beat up in July before being dealt. Hamels July had 4 starts, 17 innings and 21 ERs! He was lucky to be dealt but if you take that month out of this season over his other 28 starts his ERA was 3.06. Bauer had a career year with an unfortunate injury and would have had one of his best ERA seasons without that July so they both were great. Our judges were all over the place on this one a KO for Bauer, a 10-7 for Bauer and a 10-8 for Hamels, weird. I think Berrios vs Ray could end up like this one, a young stud taking a step up and Ray getting back on track.

Welsh's Take:

I think our Judges did a fantastic job on this one, even though it wasn't a unanimous decision to go Bauer, we had two firmly in favor. Democracy wins! It seems silly now, but these two floated in the same range, and this was very much a real debate. The book said Bauer, and it would have paid off. Bauer is really really hard to like, but if you take out all the dumb bullcrap he does and just focus on the pitcher, he was awesome last year. He's now locked himself into a top 10 overall starting pitcher spot, and it makes sense. If he can avoid injuries, I can't see a reason he doesn't repeat. Hopefully he also does more things like his 420/69 charity and less 48 straight hours of trolling a girl on twitter. Not to discount Hamels, as he was solid with the Cubs, this debate was about one pitcher taking a huge step while the other improved on his perception. I think the Carlos Martínez vs Chris Archer could mirror this one in 2019. Carlos Martinez being the pitcher that takes huge strides into top 20 or 15 territory while Archer improves his perception.

2018 Judges
Vlad Sedler - Bauer 10-7
Eddy Almaguer - Bauer KO
Doug Thorburn - Hamels 10-8

WINNER
Trevor Bauer in a 10-8 Decision

CHRISTIAN YELICH VS BILLY HAMILTON
2018

Bogman's Take:

I mean we don't need to talk about why this one didn't work out, MVP vs released from Cincinnati and hitting 9 for the Royals in 2019. The most surprising thing here is that NONE of our judges picked Yelich! We had two 10-9 Hamilton's and a Draw! I didn't even really talk up Yelich in this at all. I just down talked Hamilton and called him a one-trick pony in this one and I was right, but I didn't see an MVP season for Yelich by any stretch of the imagination. Hamilton was actually about where we expected him to be in everything EXCEPT SBs last season. While 34 is nothing to scoff at it's not worth carrying with nothing else to really add to your lineup. I don't know what debate would be even close to this from the 2019 version but if I had to pick one it would be Jose Peraza vs Jonathan Villar. Peraza would have to add a lot of power, which I don't expect but isn't out of the realm of possibility because power tends to develop last. Villar would have to fall off which has happened before so that is much more likely.

Welsh's Take:

Lol. Lmao. ROFLLMAO. Hindsight is fun, but this was a real dilemma for last year. Not that they were going next to each other, but taking roster construction and value into consideration, where would you be. Eternal hope on Hamilton right. This was a lot about possible disbelief in a major statistical upgrade in Milwaukee for Yelich, and the continued value of 50+ stolen bases for Hamilton. This couldn't have gone more south. My god, can you imagine me sitting here arguing Hamilton over Yelich, well it happened last year. I am almost certain all of the judges still were interested in Yelich, but his pre-season ADP had gotten rather lofty. Either way, sometimes we get cute, and it's also proof that we all make mistakes. All three judges picked Hamilton, and I wrote him up in defense. Smh. If I had to pick one that could resemble the magnitude of change between to players I'd go with Mondesi vs Merrifield. Nothing is more exciting than Mondesi, but this has many of the makings of the Hamilton vs Yelich from 2018. We could look back on this one and go, whoa!

2018 Judges
Paul Sporer - Hamilton 10-9
Jason Collette - DRAW
Nate Grimm - Hamilton 10-9

WINNER
Billy Hamilton in a 10-9 Decision

MOOKIE BETTS VS TREA TURNER
2018

Bogman's Take:

Well no one disappointed here really, they are both still 1st round picks but Mookie is at the spot where Trea was last year and vice versa. Mookie was unbelievably dominate last season. Betts beat Turner in 4 of 5 categories and really beat him up in AVG and HRs while playing 26 fewer games than Trea. Looks like we don't have to worry about an injury bug with Turner as he played every single game for the Nats last season. Turner wasn't able to keep up the insane pace of SBs, even dropping his 2017 total by 3 while playing 65 more games. That SB upside had all of our judges drooling, they ALL took Turner and to be honest it wasn't really that surprising. One that could be like this one for the book this year is Mondesi vs Merrifield. While not as high stakes as they aren't first round picks or anything it's a proven player vs massive SB upside.

Welsh's Take:

Everyone can still sleep at night, but this shows the worry of the one off bad average season for Mookie. He obviously came back in full force, so this isn't horrible, but crazy to see it was a clean sweep. This does make me think, and maybe this is something that is a bigger question for our podcast, but is Trea Turner one of the biggest floor players in the first round? I mean obviously there are guys we want above him, but when push comes to shove, is he the most reliable return besides Mike Trout? All it took was for Mookie was to hit .260 and people jumped off for 50+ stolen bases. Remember José Altuve? His value wasn't just locked to the stolen bases, but power. He even hit over .300 and he's going after Turner in almost every spot. Francisco Lindor is one of those guys that's jumped Turner, but is it something we should count on? There is no answer besides the result of this season, but this isn't just about Mookie's jump to clear cut number two, but maybe also how Turner's floor might be enough to be a can't miss first round pick. I think there might be a couple that qualify to mimic this debate, but I am going to pick Paul Goldschmidt vs Giancarlo Stanton. Stanton's got that floor power that'll probably keep him in the top two rounds regardless of what he does, outside of hitting sub .240. Goldschmidt though has been as valuable as number two in fantasy before, and he might be in line to return to top five value this year with the Cardinals.

2018 Judges
Paul Sporer - 10-9 Turner
Jason Collette - Turner KO
James Anderson - Turner 10-8

WINNER
Trea Turner wins in a 10-8 decision

EUGENIO SUAREZ VS ANDRELTON SIMMONS

2018

Bogman's Take:

This was an easy victory for Suárez and we can easily tell because his ADP for NFBC drafts is 150 spots higher than Simmons at 51 overall! Last season Suárez was going past 200 even after a career year in HRs, Runs and RBI. Flat out drafters were not buying into it at all but 2 of our 3 judges got this one right but it wasn't as dominating as it should have been for any of them. In all fairness though Simmons was no slouch and even upped his batting average. I think this one is the hardest to find a match one from the 2019 matchups. It seems like drafters have decided to not look at players like Suárez who keep improving and dismiss them. The closest one I can see is maybe Tim Anderson vs Jurickson Profar. Anderson has gone up in everything except average in 4 straight seasons and Profar had his best season to date last year. Maybe we should be paying attention to Anderson climbing in these categories.

Welsh's Take:

This is another one of those we look at this year, and go really? Yeah, really. Two of the three judges got it right, and one that makes me laugh because we need ro razz him, Reds fan Clay Link went against his own guy. Simmons wasn't a massive disappointment, more than anything he probably was relative to the range he was drafted at, but Suárez proved all the doubters wrong that he was fluke rather than fiction. I've got quite a few that could mirror this debate. I wanted to say Brantley vs Polanco, as I think Brantley could be in line for a big year, but he doesn't' quite have the "not buying quite in yet" feel. I'm going to go with the Donaldson vs Chapman debate. Chapman had a quietly good season. He cuts the strikeouts down a bit, builds on his average last year and pushes 30 home runs. Donaldson returns the relative value he's being drafted at, but Chapman is the guy that jumps three to four rounds the following season.

2018 Judges
Joe Pisapia - Suárez 10-8
Rob Silver - Suárez 10-9
Clay Link - Simmons 10-9

WINNER
Eugenio Suárez wins in a 10-9 decision

Top 300

Bogman	Rank	The Welsh
Mike Trout - LAA	1	Mike Trout OF - LAA
Mookie Betts - BOS	2	Mookie Betts - BOS
José Ramírez - CLE	3	José Ramírez - CLE
Francisco Lindor - CLE	4	Francisco Lindor - CLE
J.D. Martinez - BOS	5	Ronald Acuña Jr. - ATL
Nolan Arenado - COL	6	Christian Yelich - MIL
Christian Yelich - MIL	7	Nolan Arenado - COL
Ronald Acuña Jr. - ATL	8	J.D. Martinez - BOS
Trea Turner - WAS	9	Trea Turner - WAS
Manny Machado - FA	10	Bryce Harper - FA
José Altuve - HOU	11	Manny Machado - FA
Alex Bregman - HOU	12	Max Scherzer - WAS
Max Scherzer - WAS	13	José Altuve - HOU
Chris Sale - BOS	14	Alex Bregman - HOU
Jacob deGrom - NYM	15	Paul Goldschmidt - STL
Bryce Harper - FA	16	Chris Sale - BOS
Aaron Judge - NYY	17	Jacob deGrom - NYM
Giancarlo Stanton - NYY	18	Aaron Judge - NYY
Charlie Blackmon - COL	19	Giancarlo Stanton - NYY
Freddie Freeman - ATL	20	Freddie Freeman - ATL
Paul Goldschmidt - STL	21	Javier Báez - CHC
Trevor Story - COL	22	Trevor Story - COL
Javier Báez - CHC	23	Charlie Blackmon - COL
Kris Bryant - CHC	24	Kris Bryant - CHC
Carlos Correa - HOU	25	Corey Kluber - CLE
Andrew Benintendi - BOS	26	Andrew Benintendi - BOS
Corey Kluber - CLE	27	Juan Soto - WAS
Justin Verlander - HOU	28	Justin Verlander - HOU
Aaron Nola SP - PHI	29	Aaron Nola SP - PHI
Blake Snel SP - TB	30	Carlos Correa - HOU
Gerrit Cole SP - HOU	31	Blake Snel SP - TB
Vladimir Guerrero Jr. - TOR	32	Anthony Rizzo - CHC
Juan Soto - WAS	33	Clayton Kershaw - LAD
Luis Severino - NYY	34	Gerrit Cole SP - HOU
Clayton Kershaw - LAD	35	Starling Marté - PIT
Anthony Rizzo - CHC	36	Whit Merrifield - KC
Whit Merrifield - KC	37	Rhys Hoskins - PHI
Carlos Carrasco - CLE	38	Luis Severino - NYY
Noah Syndergaard - NYM	39	Khris Davis - OAK
Trevor Bauer - CLE	40	Carlos Carrasco - CLE
Starling Marté - PIT	41	Noah Syndergaard - NYM
Cody Bellinger - LAD	42	Cody Bellinger - LAD
Khris Davis - OAK	43	Anthony Rendon - WAS
Walker Buehler - LAD	44	Vladimir Guerrero Jr. - TOR
Anthony Rendon - WAS	45	George Springer - HOU
Rhys Hoskins - PHI	46	Trevor Bauer - CLE
Adalberto Mondesi - KC	47	Walker Buehler - LAD
Eugenio Suárez - CIN	48	Xander Bogaerts - BOS
Xander Bogaerts - BOS	49	Joey Votto - CIN
Gleyber Torres - NYY	50	Gleyber Torres - NYY

Bogman	Rank	The Welsh
Ozzie Albies - ATL	51	Adalberto Mondesi - KC
Patrick Corbin - WAS	52	Ozzie Albies - ATL
Miguel Andújar - NYY	53	Eugenio Suárez - CIN
Matt Carpenter - STL	54	Corey Seager - LAD
George Springer - HOU	55	James Paxton - NYY
Joey Votto - CIN	56	Stephen Strasburg - WAS
Tommy Pham - TB	57	Matt Carpenter - STL
Jesús Aguilar - MIL	58	Patrick Corbin - WAS
David Price - BOS	59	Lorenzo Cain - MIL
James Paxton - NYY	60	Justin Upton - LAA
Zack Greinke - ARI	61	Miguel Andújar - NYY
Mike Clevinger - CLE	62	Edwin Díaz - NYM
Marcell Ozuna - STL	63	Jean Segura - PHI
Lorenzo Cain - MIL	64	José Abreu - CWS
Edwin Díaz - NYM	65	Marcell Ozuna - STL
German Márquez - COL	66	Zack Greinke - ARI
Stephen Strasburg - WAS	67	A.J. Pollock - LAD
Jack Flaherty - STL	68	Tommy Pham - TB
Carlos Martínez - STL	69	Mike Clevinger - CLE
Mitch Haniger - SEA	70	Madison Bumgarner - SF
Wil Myers - SD	71	David Dahl - COL
Nicholas Castellanos - DET	72	Matt Chapman - OAK
Justin Upton - LAA	73	Jack Flaherty - STL
José Abreu - CWS	74	Scooter Gennett - CIN
Josh Donaldson - ATL	75	Nicholas Castellanos - DET
Jean Segura - PHI	76	Kenley Jansen - LAD
Corey Seager - LAD	77	Craig Kimbrel - FA
José Berrios - MIN	78	Gary Sánchez - NYY
Jameson Taillon - PIT	79	Josh Donaldson - ATL
Michael Brantley - HOU	80	Nelson Cruz - MIN
Michael Conforto - NYM	81	Wil Myers - SD
Víctor Robles - WAS	82	Jameson Taillon - PIT
Madison Bumgarner - SF	83	Blake Treinen - OAK
Blake Treinen - OAK	84	Yasiel Puig - CIN
Craig Kimbrel - FA	85	Eddie Rosario - MIN
Mike Foltynewicz - ATL	86	Mitch Haniger - SEA
Masahiro Tanaka - NYY	87	Víctor Robles - WAS
Scooter Gennett - CIN	88	David Price - BOS
Aroldis Chapman - NYY	89	Daniel Murphy - COL
Kenley Jansen - LAD	90	Michael Brantley - HOU
J.T. Realmuto - MIA	91	José Berrios - MIN
Gary Sánchez - NYY	92	Aroldis Chapman - NYY
Matt Chapman - OAK	93	Matt Olson - OAK
Matt Olson - OAK	94	J.T. Realmuto - MIA
Eddie Rosario - MIN	95	Mike Foltynewicz - ATL
David Peralta - ARI	96	Eloy Jimenez - CWS
Aaron Hicks - NYY	97	Zack Wheeler - NYM
Nelson Cruz - MIN	98	Justin Turner - LAD
Zack Wheeler - NYM	99	Michael Conforto - NYM
Edwin Encarnación - SEA	100	German Márquez - COL

Bogman	Rank	The Welsh
Joey Gallo - TEX	101	Travis Shaw - MIL
José Peraza - CIN	102	Max Muncy - LAD
Daniel Murphy - COL	103	Roberto Osuna - HOU
Robbie Ray - ARI	104	Felipe Vázquez - PIT
Miles Mikolas - STL	105	Mallex Smith - SEA
Luis Castillo SP- CIN	106	Edwin Encarnación - SEA
Yu Darvish - CHC	107	Raisel Iglesias - CIN
Travis Shaw - MIL	108	Carlos Martínez - STL
Robinson Canó - NYM	109	Josh Hader - MIL
Tim Anderson - CWS	110	Robbie Ray - ARI
Jurickson Profar - OAK	111	Luis Castillo SP- CIN
Ian Desmond - COL	112	Joey Gallo - TEX
Rafael Devers - BOS	113	José Peraza - CIN
Chris Archer - PIT	114	Miles Mikolas - STL
Cole Hamels - CHC	115	Brad Hand - CLE
Kyle Hendricks - CHC	116	Dee Gordon - SEA
A.J. Pollock - LAD	117	Andrew McCutchen - PHI
Max Muncy - LAD	118	Jesús Aguilar - MIL
Eloy Jimenez - CWS	119	Rougned Odor - TEX
Stephen Piscotty - OAK	120	Robinson Canó - NYM
Ender Inciarte - ATL	121	Chris Archer - PIT
Mallex Smith - SEA	122	Aaron Hicks - NYY
Eduardo Rodríguez - BOS	123	David Peralta - ARI
Rougned Odor - TEX	124	Masahiro Tanaka - NYY
Yoan Moncada - CWS	125	Sean Doolittle - WAS
Felipe Vázquez - PIT	126	Tim Anderson - CWS
Josh Hader - MIL	127	Ender Inciarte - ATL
Roberto Osuna - HOU	128	Nomar Mazara - TEX
Sean Doolittle - WAS	129	Brian Dozier - WAS
Brad Hand - CLE	130	Jonathan Villar - BAL
Raisel Iglesias - CIN	131	Jurickson Profar - OAK
Mike Moustakas - FA	132	Charlie Morton - TB
Andrew McCutchen - PHI	133	Kyle Hendricks - CHC
Brandon Nimmo - NYM	134	Yoan Moncada - CWS
Eduardo Escobar -ARI	135	Miguel Cabrera - DET
Miguel Cabrera - DET	136	Ian Desmond - COL
Justin Turner - LAD	137	Yu Darvish - CHC
Yasiel Puig - CIN	138	Rafael Devers - BOS
Nomar Mazara - TEX	139	Eduardo Rodríguez - BOS
David Dahl - COL	140	Salvador Pérez - KC
J.A. Happ - NYY	141	Kirby Yates -SD
Charlie Morton - TB	142	Ken Giles - HOU
Josh James - HOU	143	J.A. Happ - NYY
Kyle Freeland - COL	144	Dallas Keuchel - FA
Rick Porcello - BOS	145	Kyle Freeland - COL
Jonathan Villar - BAL	146	Willson Contreras - CHC
César Hernández - PHI	147	Elvis Andrus - TEX
Tyler Glasnow - TB	148	Mike Moustakas - FA
Dee Gordon - SEA	149	Buster Posey - SF
Paul DeJong - STL	150	Harrison Bader - STL

Bogman	Rank	The Welsh
Willson Contreras - CHC	151	Brandon Nimmo - NYM
Ken Giles - HOU	152	Amed Rosario - NYM
Kirby Yates -SD	153	Tyler Glasnow - TB
Wade Davis - COL	154	Nick Pivetta - PHI
Jordan Hicks - STL	155	Wilson Ramos - NYM
José Leclerc - TEX	156	César Hernández - PHI
Corey Knebel - MIL	157	Eric Hosmer - SD
Brian Dozier - WAS	158	Ryan Braun - MIL
Byron Buxton - MIN	159	Byron Buxton - MIN
Kyle Schwarber - CHC	160	Cole Hamels - CHC
Austin Meadows - TB	161	Wade Davis - COL
Corey Dickerson - PIT	162	Shohei Ohtani - LAA
Hunter Renfroe - SD	163	Gregory Polanco- PIT
Adam Jones - BAL	164	Rich Hill - LAD
Gregory Polanco- PIT	165	Yusei Kikuchi - SEA
Chris Taylor - LAD	166	Kyle Schwarber - CHC
Buster Posey - SF	167	Billy Hamilton - KC
Yadier Molina - STL	168	José Leclerc - TEX
Shane Bieber - CLE	169	Corey Knebel - MIL
Nick Pivetta - PHI	170	Jesse Winker - CIN
Jon Lester - CHC	171	Andrew Heaney - LAA
Jon Gray - COL	172	Jonathan Schoop - MIN
Andrew Heaney - LAA	173	Justin Smoak - TOR
Steven Matz - NYM	174	DJ LeMahieu - NYY
Nathan Eovaldi - BOS	175	Jon Lester - CHC
José Quintana - CHC	176	Yasmani Grandal - MIL
Dallas Keuchel - FA	177	Austin Meadows - TB
Kevin Gausman - ATL	178	Nathan Eovaldi - BOS
Yusei Kikuchi - SEA	179	Shin-Soo Choo - TEX
Salvador Pérez - KC	180	Adam Jones - BAL
Wilson Ramos - NYM	181	Eduardo Escobar -ARI
Yasmani Grandal - MIL	182	Rick Porcello - BOS
Elvis Andrus - TEX	183	José Quintana - CHC
Jorge Polanco - MIN	184	Shane Bieber - CLE
Willy Adames - TB	185	Yuli Gurriel - HOU
Marcus Semien - OAK	186	Paul DeJong - STL
Miguel Sanó - MIN	187	Hunter Renfroe - SD
Jake Lamb - ARI	188	Jorge Polanco - MIN
Kyle Seager - SEA	189	Stephen Piscotty - OAK
Jed Lowrie - NYM	180	Miguel Sanó - MIN
Maikel Franco - PHI	191	David Robertson - PHI
Joey Wendle - TB	192	Andrew Miller - STL
Peter Alonso - NYM	193	Jed Lowrie - NYM
C.J. Cron - MIN	194	Willy Adames - TB
Yuli Gurriel - HOU	195	Kyle Seager - SEA
DJ LeMahieu - NYY	196	Kevin Gausman - ATL
Andrelton Simmons - LAA	197	Alex Wood - CIN
Garrett Hampson - COL	198	Tyler Skaggs - LAA
Ryan Braun - MIL	199	Josh James - HOU
Nick Senzel - CIN	200	Nick Senzel - CIN

Bogman	Rank	The Welsh
Shin-Soo Choo - TEX	201	Jake Arrieta - PHI
Trey Mancini - BAL	202	Garrett Hampson - COL
Max Kepler - MIN	203	Jake Bauers - CLE
Kendrys Morales - TOR	204	Jake Lamb - ARI
Amed Rosario - NYM	205	Yadier Molina - STL
Jesse Winker - CIN	206	Zack Godley - ARI
Avisaíl Garcia - TB	207	Carlos Santana - CLE
Adam Eaton - WAS	208	Adam Eaton - WAS
Billy Hamilton - KC	209	Peter Alonso - NYM
Shohei Ohtani - LAA	210	Cody Allen - LAA
Luke Voit - NYY	211	José Alvarado - TB
Eric Hosmer - SD	212	Luis Urias - SD
Carlos Santana - CLE	213	Joey Wendle - TB
Alex Reyes - STL	214	Odúbel Herrera - PHI
Justin Smoak - TOR	215	Manuel Margot - SD
Tyler White - HOU	216	Luke Voit - NYY
Zack Godley - ARI	217	Hyun-Jin Ryu - LAD
Marco Gonzales - SEA	218	José Martínez - STL
Alex Wood - CIN	219	Max Kepler - MIN
Reynaldo López - CWS	220	Steven Souza Jr. - ARI
Jake Arrieta - PHI	221	Ian Happ - CHC
Luke Weaver - ARI	222	Jackie Bradley Jr. - BOS
Tyler Skaggs - LAA	223	Marcus Semien - OAK
Joey Lucchesi - SD	224	Andrelton Simmons - LAA
Kenta Maeda - LAD	225	Chris Taylor - LAD
Joe Musgrove - PIT	226	Danny Jansen - TOR
Marcus Stroman - TOR	227	Ramón Laureano - OAK
Julio Teheran - ATL	228	Ketel Marte - ARI
Jhoulys Chacín - MIL	229	Archie Bradley - ARI
Rich Hill - LAD	230	Jon Gray - COL
Hyun-Jin Ryu - LAD	231	Trey Mancini - BAL
David Robertson - PHI	232	Arodys Vizcaíno - ATL
José Alvarado - TB	233	A.J. Minter - ATL
Arodys Vizcaíno - ATL	234	Mike Soroka - ATL
Asdrúbal Cabrera - TEX	235	Kendrys Morales - TOR
Jonathan Schoop - MIN	236	Maikel Franco - PHI
Luis Urias - SD	237	Tyler White - HOU
Ketel Marte - ARI	238	Jordan Hicks - STL
Lourdes Gurriel Jr. - TOR	239	Marwin González - FA
Steven Souza Jr. - ARI	240	Lourdes Gurriel Jr. - TOR
Brett Gardner - NYY	241	Yonder Alonso - CWS
Matt Kemp - CIN	242	Matt Kemp - CIN
Harrison Bader - STL	243	Alex Reyes - STL
Ramón Laureano - OAK	244	Kyle Tucker - HOU
Jackie Bradley Jr. - BOS	245	Will Smith - SF
Yonder Alonso - CWS	246	Josh Bell - PIT
Ryan Zimmerman - WAS	247	Franmil Reyes - SD
Mitch Moreland - BOS	248	Avisaíl Garcia - TB
Niko Goodrum - DET	249	Sean Newcomb - ATL
Jay Bruce - SEA	250	Kelvin Herrera - CWS

Bogman	Rank	The Welsh
Archie Bradley - ARI	251	Seranthony Dominguez - PHI
Jeimer Candelario - DET	252	Marcus Stroman - TOR
Daniel Palka - CWS	253	C.J. Cron - MIN
Randal Grichuk - TOR	254	Brett Gardner - NYY
Ian Happ - CHC	255	Steven Matz - NYM
Ian Kinsler - SD	256	Jesus Luzardo - OAK
Marwin González - FA	257	Mychal Givens - BAL
Odúbel Herrera - PHI	258	Corey Dickerson - PIT
Nick Markakis - ATL	259	Didi Gregorius - NYY
Christin Stewart - DET	260	Forrest Whitley - HOU
Franmil Reyes - SD	261	Niko Goodrum - DET
Jorge Soler - KC	262	Luke Weaver - ARI
Brian Anderson - MIA	263	Kevin Kiermaier OF
Kyle Tucker - HOU	264	Drew Steckenrider - MIA
Andrew Miller - STL	265	Nick Markakis - ATL
Shane Greene - DET	266	Joc Pederson - LAD
Will Smith - SF	267	Yan Gomes - CLE
Dereck Rodríguez - SF	268	Willians Astudillo - MIN
Sean Newcomb - ATL	269	Michael Wacha -STL
Forrest Whitley - HOU	270	Dereck Rodríguez - SF
Cody Allen - LAA	271	Joey Lucchesi - SD
A.J. Minter - ATL	272	Mitch Moreland - BOS
Drew Steckenrider - MIA	273	Ryan Zimmerman - WAS
Brandon Morrow - CHC	274	Kenta Maeda - LAD
Seranthony Dominguez - PHI	275	Christin Stewart - DET
Brandon Woodruff - MIL	276	Tyler O'Neill - STL
Carlos Rodón - CWS	277	Jimmy Nelson - MIL
Trevor Williams - PIT	278	Jeff McNeil - NYM
Jake Bauers - CLE	279	Greg Holland - ARI
Josh Bell - PIT	280	Delino DeShields - TEX
Jesus Luzardo - OAK	281	Sonny Gray - CIN
Mike Soroka - ATL	282	Ian Kinsler - SD
Starlin Castro - MIA	283	Shane Greene - DET
Danny Jansen - TOR	284	Dansby Swanson - ATL
Jorge Alfaro - PHI	285	Jhoulys Chacin - MIL
Mychal Givens - BAL	286	Jay Bruce - SEA
Alex Colome - CWS	287	Yandy Díaz - TB
Kelvin Herrera - CWS	288	Matt Harvey - LAA
Joc Pederson - LAD	289	Jorge Soler - KC
Kevin Kiermaier OF	290	Franchy Cordero- SD
Willians Astudillo - MIN	291	Asdrúbal Cabrera - TEX
Yan Gomes - CLE	292	Alex Verdugo - LAD
Francisco Mejía - SD	293	Jeimer Candelario - DET
Matt Harvey - LAA	294	Welington Castillo- CWS
Gio Gonzalez - FA	295	Dellin Betances-NYY
Matthew Boyd - DET	296	Marco Gonzales - SEA
Sonny Gray - CIN	297	Kyle Gibson - MIN
Michael Wacha -STL	298	Gio Gonzalez - FA
Jake Odorizzi - MIN	299	Reynaldo López - CWS
Jeff Samardzija - SF	300	Fernando Tatis Jr. - SD

Made in the USA
Lexington, KY
11 February 2019